START AT THE END

START AT
THE END

//

HOW TO BUILD PRODUCTS
THAT CHANGE BEHAVIOR

Matt Wallaert

PORTFOLIO / PENGUIN

PORTFOLIO/PENGUIN
An imprint of Penguin Random House LLC
penguinrandomhouse.com

Copyright © 2019 by Matt Wallaert

Most Portfolio books are available at a discount when purchased in quantity for sales promotions or corporate use. Special editions, which include personalized covers, excerpts, and corporate imprints, can be created when purchased in large quantities. For more information, please call (212) 572-2232 or e-mail specialmarkets@penguinrandomhouse.com. Your local bookstore can also assist with discounted bulk purchases using the Penguin Random House corporate Business-to-Business program. For assistance in locating a participating retailer, e-mail B2B@penguinrandomhouse.com.

ISBN 9780525534426 (hardcover)
ISBN 9780525534433 (ebook)

Printed in the United States of America
10 9 8 7 6 5 4 3 2 1

BOOK DESIGN BY MEIGHAN CAVANAUGH

*Penguin is committed to publishing works of quality and integrity.
In that spirit, we are proud to offer this book to our readers;
however, the story, the experiences, and the words are the author's alone.*

For Bear

Far and away the best prize that life has to offer is the chance to work hard at work worth doing.

—Teddy Roosevelt

CONTENTS

//

Acknowledgments *xi*

Introduction *xv*

PART 1

THE BASICS OF BEHAVIOR CHANGE

1. The Intervention Design Process *3*

2. Potential Insights and Insight Validation *13*

3. Behavioral Statement *27*

4. Pressure Mapping and Pressure Validation *51*

5. Intervention Design and Intervention
   Selection *69*

6. **Ethical Check** *83*

7. **Pilot and Pilot Validation, Test and Test Validation, Scale Decision and Continuous Measurement** *99*

8. **The End of the Beginning** *123*

PART 2

ADVANCED BEHAVIOR CHANGE

9. **Priming, Moderation, and Mediation** *131*

10. **Optimum Cognition** *145*

11. **Uniqueness and Belonging** *157*

12. **Special Factors of Inhibiting Pressures** *179*

13. **Competing Behaviors** *185*

14. **Eliminating and Replacing Behavior** *191*

15. **Mini Case Studies** *197*

Notes *219*

Index *223*

ACKNOWLEDGMENTS

Nothing in this book is entirely original. The content relies on a long history of studies done by researchers in social psychology and other sciences, and on the experiences of hundreds of talented people in organizations that span the globe. That I've added some structure and process to make their research and experience easier to apply is just another small contribution in a line of small contributions that have led and will lead to a better world.

The point of the book is to help you add your own contribution. Remember, there have been a few giants, but it is mostly iteration that has gotten us this far. I don't believe that behavior-change practices should be kept in proprietary silos, deployed only by a dark cabal of consultants. The world gets better when we collectively get better at making it that way.

I started my career in product development in the late 2000s, after leaving grad school to own product at Thrive, a personal finance startup that we eventually sold to Lending Tree. But the real seeds of the process I'll lay out here started long before I was born, with Kurt Lewin and his work on field theory (which I've turned vertically and called competing pressures). His work was so long in the tooth that we didn't read it when I was in school, but Andrew Ward (my undergraduate adviser at Swarthmore, along with Barry Schwartz) did, and he gave me a MacDonald paper[1] that was really the catalyst for my continued work on behavior change. The authors started, as so many good scientists do, with a brain teaser: is there a set of conditions in which a drunk person would be more likely to have safe sex than a sober person?

The answer turned out to be a hand stamp that said "AIDS Kills." Because alcohol limits brain function, drunk people tend to focus on the most obvious things in their environment. And when one of those is a scary message about AIDS, they report a greater desire to have safe sex than sober people do. The stamp is a pressure—something that causes behavior to be more or less likely. MacDonald's paper inspired Ward and his frequent collaborator Traci Mann to posit a more generalized model of attentional myopia.[2] It showed that by selectively narrowing attention, they could change a wide variety of behaviors, like eating more or less or being more or less aggressive toward others. In a similar study I published with them, we showed that you could change the behavior of college students who smoked by putting a sticker on their lighter reminding them that "Smoking Kills"—just like MacDonald's AIDS stamp.[3] Students were asked to use the lighter when they wanted to smoke, but some of them had an additional task of counting backward by tens. The students whose brains were distracted by counting smoked less, because their overall attention became myopic— they were disproportionately affected by the warning sticker on the lighter.

That was the seed for me. If narrowing attention could change the strength of pressures and thus change behavior, there must be other ways to modify those pressures. With conscious intent and deliberate outcome, pressures could be designed for and their effects altered to create a different world. That seed became this book.

If this book is a startup, that is the founding story. It is also the most research papers you'll see cited in a single section for the rest of this book; I'll try to stick with practical examples over lab studies whenever possible. But I do want to acknowledge the work of a few people before abandoning citation.

I would never have become a social psychologist if not for Andrew Ward and Barry Schwartz, who managed to see past the arrogance of youth to the curiosity that frequently lies underneath. Stef Sugar, continues to put up with the more advanced arrogance of my middle age. My parents and brother just put up with me, period. Graham Moore showed me what it is to write a book. Avi Karnani took a bet on me at Thrive and again with Churnless, and we'll eventually find an excuse to do it again. Stefan Weitz and Adam Sohn brought me to Microsoft; I'll work for Anna Roth anytime. Dan Storms has talked about product with me way, way too much. Adam Grant was the first person to ever put me in a book and constantly reminds me about my gender blind spot. Jennifer Kurdyla wrote this down. The list goes on, but it would not be complete without my editor at Penguin, Merry Sun, who was the only publisher ever to talk me into agreeing to write this down. Many tried and failed (another publisher asked me to stop giving free talks and only agree to speak if organizers guaranteed a certain number of books sold; welcome to modern publishing); she succeeded by being direct, honest, and clear that I didn't have to do anything but write the book I wanted to write.

But above all others, it is my son, Bear, who catalyzed my writing. I simply couldn't keep leaving him to explain it in talk after talk after talk around the world. When this is published, I will have the supreme pleasure of turning down speaking requests by saying, "I'm playing with my son; go read the book." I look forward to this, and my greatest pleasure is knowing that he does too.

INTRODUCTION

Humans are born behavioral scientists. From our very first cry, we begin to shape what others do by exerting pressure—bawl and they feed us, coo and they snuggle us. And we are similarly shaped by the pressures of others. We're taught how to speak, dress, and act both explicitly and implicitly, through millions of subtle interactions with people and our environment. We change the behavior of others naturally and constantly, simply by being alive and part of a larger population.

This natural tendency toward behavior change manifests as our creative drive. Because we're wired to influence what others do, we're constantly creating to get what we want. As a consequence, nearly everything we come in contact with is constructed to shape behavior. Sidewalks tell us to walk here and not there. Movies tell us to laugh or to cry. Wearing a tie says, "Call me Mr. Tibbs!" while a Hawaiian shirt elicits a first name.

Yet we rarely connect our desire to create with the goal of behavior change. At most companies, the decision-making process behind what we build still looks like an episode of *Mad Men*: people, generally white and male and lacking any expertise other than privilege, throw ideas out until one of them sounds sexy enough, and that's what gets built. The rationalization is entirely post hoc, created simply to support an idea that a decision maker has already fallen in love with.

Hence the modern "why we make what we make" vision statement. No mention of behavior, no acceptance of the goal of creation, just a mélange of high-def puff pieces designed to appeal to our need to both stand out and fit in. Even at companies that ought to know better, we have fetishized the process over its outcome and a stylish product over its intended behavior change. Then we attempt to make up for it by shouting as loudly as possible about how cool our products are, hoping to create a motivation where none previously existed. What an awful waste.

Advertising accounts for more than 1 percent of the U.S. gross domestic product: $220 billion of spend to compensate for a process that doesn't consider behavior change its central aim. Instead of basic psychology, we use brute force to fuel a massive competition for attention, and our world is worse off because of it. Instead of starting at the end—a clearly described behavior that is the explicit goal of creation—our method of design has come to embrace the sexy sell and the need to sound good instead of be good. We have so deeply internalized product marketing that we make products with the advertisements in mind.

If that sounds great and you still want to live in a *Mad Men* world, it's not too late to turn a blind eye. No one is forcing you to read this book and start changing behavior. Amazon has a very generous return policy. I encourage regifting—it is the ultimate environmentalism.

But if you believe this system is unsustainable and want to get busy doing something different, good news: you've come to the right place. Here we'll prioritize outcome over process, while recognizing that some processes get you better outcomes. We'll put behavior change first by starting at the end.

Start at the End: Behavior Change as a Different, Better Kind of Why

The iPhone has been held up as the pinnacle of vision, inspiration, and creativity—a modern miracle courtesy of the Don Drapers of the world that defined the quintessential Apple *why?* as challenging the status quo in everything the company does. The only problem with that narrative is it has very little to do with what made the iPhone successful while other status quo challengers (the Kin, anyone?) fell utterly flat.

What made the iPhone work is really two *why*s that together bridged what psychologists call a counterfactual world—the world that doesn't exist but could—with the one we live in. Apple imagined a world in which people used their phones everywhere, all the time, to honor a vast range of motivations. Then it built a device that guided people to do that, not by "challenging the status quo" in every aspect but by asking "*Why* would people want to do that in the first place?" and "*Why* aren't they doing it already?"

Those two questions are at the heart of this book. The first maps motivation to the conditions that make behavior more likely, called promoting pressures. The second helps us understand the factors (like "AIDS kills" stamps) that make the behavior less likely, called inhibiting pressures. Identifying and consciously influencing the strength of those pressures is the basis of designing for behavior change, codified here as the Intervention Design Process (IDP)—interventions being the things we build to change the pressures and thus the resultant behaviors. The rest of the book, in one way or another, is about how to design with these pressures in mind to create interventions that work, where "work" means "change behavior" in ways that we can measure.

I'll confess that even though I opened with a condemnation of advertising, ad budgets alone probably wouldn't have led me to this book. Instead, I'm the most clichéd of writers: no zealot like a convert. I created the IDP because I needed it.

By training I'm a social psychologist, a field that frequently tries to inhabit the counterfactual world. Indeed, what is a lab experiment but the attempt to create a reality precisely like this one but where one key thing is changed such that it changes everything else around it? Such is the process of science: you attempt to fix all known variables so that you can understand the cause and effect of changing just one.

As a budding academic with a drive to make the world a better place—a *why* imprinted on me by my parents—I was convinced that social psychology was the secret to behavior. I had gone to college, discovered the field and nearly a hundred years of research on behavior change, and become fascinated by the practical applications of what we knew about why we do what we do. For years my passion trumped my need for daylight, and I ran literally hundreds of studies, packing eight or ten experiments into the same session and borrowing other researchers' slots so I could start to tease out more of the rules that determined behavior. By the time I went off to a social psychology PhD program, I had papers in the pipeline and a strong academic career in front of me.

In grad school I built myself a palace in that counterfactual world, trying to unlock a bridge to better behavior through scholarship. But when I picked my head up and looked at the results of my work, I discovered to my dismay that a lifetime of research and peer-reviewed papers was less likely to have lasting impact on the lives of others than building even a moderately successful product. So I built one. And then another and another and so on, for roughly the next ten years, because creation is one of the single best ways to better the world.

And the whole time, people looked at me like I was an alien. I was too applied for the pure psychologists (a very famous social psychologist once called me before offering me a graduate school fellowship to make sure I understood that theirs was a *research* department; he knew before I did that academia wasn't right for me, and I was just too stubborn to listen) but far too experimental and insistent on scientific rigor for the corporate folks (the number of execs who think a focus group counts as an experiment is shocking). As I transitioned into startups and the business world, it felt like every meeting required a mini lecture on what behavioral science was and, because I hadn't yet developed a meaningful framework to get others to do what I was doing naturally, all of my early product wins seemed more like magic than science, because I couldn't explain where they were coming from.

In 2002 Daniel Kahneman did us all a huge favor by winning the Nobel Prize (in economics—there is no Nobel for psychology, so we had to steal theirs). That paved the way for a plethora of popular-science books and TED talks about behavioral science by Angela Duckworth and Dan Ariely and others, collectively bringing the cognitive processes behind our decisions and habits into the mainstream. Behavior change started having its fifteen minutes of fame (which is a profoundly weird thing to say about a science).

Except it never really got famous enough to be ubiquitous, even more than fifteen years after Danny's Nobel Prize. Despite a drumbeat of attention around behavioral science, I'm still one of only a few Chief Behavioral Officers in the world. People may be fascinated enough by behavioral science to read about it (which is probably why my publisher is willing to bankroll this book), but they have been very slow to adopt it. I maintain an employable status mostly because people still don't see themselves as able to apply behavioral science without expert guidance.

I blame academia. As a field, we've done a spectacularly bad job of emerging from our ivory towers and getting serious about the application of what we discover. There are precious few simple but effective frameworks available to help people apply behavioral science. And even those few who have tried to create them are credential obsessed, fixating on peer-reviewed papers over practicality and p-values over effect sizes.

The sad part of this lag in application is that we are better equipped to change behavior than ever. Advances in social psychology and behavioral economics have greatly increased our ability to understand why people do what they do and thus to intervene to create change. Couple this knowledge with the ability to deploy interventions via random assignment through connected devices and the internet, and data sensors that allow us to measure those interventions, and you've got a recipe for practical behavior change at a scale never before seen.

Hence this book. I'm a zealot for behavior change, in part because of my conversion from a gnostic world to an applied one. I passionately want you to believe in a specific counterfactual world—the one with systematic behavior change at the center of the creation process—and adopt it as your own. Because if enough of us do that, the counterfactual world becomes the real one. Then we can start to transition other worlds into reality, ones where we don't waste most of our creative energy on advertising (and even more of our planetary resources on stuff we throw out); where sidewalks lead us where we want to go; where more people wear Hawaiian shirts, and Mr. Tibbs gets respect not because Sidney Poitier has an epic unblinking stare but automatically. Racism, sexism, poverty, the environment—I believe designing for behavior change is our best weapon in the war on our own self-destruction.

To that end, I give you the IDP, which is framework and not gospel. It is meant to be broadly applicable across industries, to scale up to behavior change at the global level and down to controlling your personal junk-food habits, and to be bias reducing in nature by relying on a science-like process.

Try to see this book as an example of how it can be done; your job is to find the modifications that make it work in your environment.

Part 1 walks you through the IDP step by step. It is Behavior Change 101, and if you plan to implement the IDP at scale, it is the half of the book that you'll want everyone to read and commit to before you start, because it focuses on process over theory. And if you stop at Part 1, you can still be good at this work.

The difference between a junior and a senior behavioral scientist isn't instinct or talent; it is experience. And so Part 2 is a cheat sheet of what I've learned from doing this work for the past fifteen years. It is structured as a series of independent deep dives; like a good album, they are laid out in an order that makes sense to me, but unlike the chapters of Part 1, you don't need to read them all or in the order I've placed them for your reading to be valuable. And at times they might not make much sense until you've started changing behavior for yourself, so Part 2 may be something you'll need to revisit again after you've tried implementing the IDP.

///////////////

As we approach the end of this lengthy intro, I'll warn you that what follows is uncharted territory. Here there be monsters—including cursing, examples that involve unpleasant things, and open mockery of sexist, racist, and otherwise unacceptable behaviors, with an acknowledgment that I have been and will continue to be guilty of all of them. I take this tone consciously, because the mode in which such business books (the category my editor says this falls into) are written usually alienates and discourages those who most need them. Yes, I could probably write a book without cursing, but why would I want to do that? This book is authentically mine, and if you have issues with the voice in it, please direct those criticisms squarely at me.

Because in a book about challenging the prevailing notion of why we behave the way we do, it is important for us to question our own assumptions about what kind of package behavior change will come in. It will curse and use language in ways that we may not consider professional. It won't always be white and male and slim and in a suit; I am neither its ambassador nor its prototype. Behavior change will fuck with you, and if you're any good at it, you'll learn to love that.

One more egalitarian note, to go with the cursing: You don't need a PhD. I promise you, you don't need a PhD. I don't have a PhD and I'm as close to an expert as we have! If behavior is your outcome and science is your process, you are a behavioral scientist. Janitors can be behavioral scientists, if they start hacking on how to make men pee in the fucking urinal instead of on the floor (the real reason for urinal cakes: they're just for target practice). Getting a PhD will make you better at making science your process and behavior your outcome simply through repetition, but there are many ways to practice; and remember, all we care about here is the behavior change you produce.

But even something so egalitarian needs guardrails. Apple wasn't out to create a world of neck-craning device addicts; it wasn't about habit (Facebook, *cough cough*; the tobacco industry, *cough up a lung*), and neither is this book. Yes, there is cerebral chemistry that gets us hooked (or unhooked, for that matter) on products. Designing for habit and the reprogramming of the brain is simply unethical, as it explicitly circumvents our intentions by exploiting the brain's need to save cognitive resources and create shortcuts. Designing for behavior change is about creating the conditions that allow us to act on our original motivations. Sometimes, like a well-worn path, habits do arise out of those new, frequent behaviors, but only as a result of natural repetition, not from design.

So this book isn't neuroscience. It also isn't an ethical rant. I have an issue with designing for habit, but I also have issues with sexist CEOs (Travis is and always will be responsible for the systematic sexism that went down on his watch at Uber) and spending more than two minutes shopping for clothes; I'll do my best to call out my biases where they crop up and trust you to discount for them as you see fit. Where research is important, I will cite it, although you should not expect a book of footnotes, nor should you believe any book simply because it has them; I want you to benefit from science but don't require that you worship at its altar. And likewise, when companies or products have done behavior change well, I will call out what they did. These are not endorsements of their business goals or leaders, but rather illustrations meant to help change your behavior so you can change the behaviors of others.

Finally, some important notes about dualities. It is fundamentally true that any pressure that can be used to make behavior more likely can also be used to make it less likely; in the same way that stronger promoting or weaker inhibiting pressures make a behavior more likely, weaker promoting or stronger inhibiting pressures make it less likely. So while the book uses the general frame of getting people to do things, the methods it describes can also be used for getting people to not do them. This is a generalizable model, and it is only for linguistic ease that I write it directionally, so remember it works both ways.

There is another, more fundamental duality here, one that comes with any powerful framework (and Spider-Man comics): this book can be used for good or ill. The same changes we make to decrease smoking can be reversed to increase smoking (and have been). Early in my academic career, I realized that the papers I was writing about how to help people spend less and save more could, in the wrong hands, be used to encourage them do the opposite. What I've learned over time is that behavior change is a war between the vested interests on both sides of a behavioral outcome. This war is usually won by big companies with deep pockets, simply because they have more ability to brute-force behavior change (and because $200 billion of ad spend is a pretty big promoting pressure).

But take heart, for I come to you at the turning of the tide. This book is my attempt at guerrilla warfare. There is a lyric from the British rapper The Streets that I love; take it as a war cry:

He might get the ace or the top one
So organize your twos and threes into a run
And then you'll have fucked him, son

The big companies that are likely to use behavior change to sell more cigarettes, bullets, or sugar have stacked the deck in their favor, just like The Streets's privileged elite who always get the high cards. But their size tends to increase their inertia, making change more difficult as they fight to keep their curated hierarchies. They're stuck with *Mad Men*, while advances in thinking favor the small and nimble because they are quickest to pivot. Those of us who want to fight smoking or violence or obesity will never have the ad budget, but by democratizing the process by which systematic behavior change occurs, we can fight smarter. It is on us to line up those twos and threes and to do it better and more quickly than big companies can. This book isn't explicitly a manifesto, but feel free to read it as one.

And it isn't just about conscious good versus conscious evil. Again, as with anything powerful, you can have the best of intentions and still do serious harm if you use this process irresponsibly. I've done it before and I'll likely do it again. So while there is a section specifically on ethics later, always remember that behavior change is best done with a transparent goal that is clear and shared by both you and those whose behaviors you seek to change. If you are unsure, then you need to stop, discuss, and revise. I can't force you to be careful, but I can ask it of you.

And now I need to take my own advice. This book is the result of the process described herein and thus has an explicit behavioral outcome in mind: when you want to change the world, and you've read this book, you will design explicitly toward a behavioral goal and apply a systematic method to implementing interventions that achieve it. And in doing so, you will not only be more effective at changing behaviors but also accelerate our collective advancement toward a better world, so that is how I'll measure the book's success as an intervention. A better world and nothing less.

All clear? In the immortal words of Marvin Gaye, let's get it on.

PART 1

///

THE BASICS
OF BEHAVIOR
CHANGE

1.

THE INTERVENTION DESIGN PROCESS

When we want to change behavior, we start with a potential insight—an observation about the distance between our current world and the counterfactual one in which we want to live. We then validate the insight and flesh it out into a behavioral statement, which we use to map the pressures that are creating the current state of the behavior and thus are the levers we push to change it. After we've validated the pressures, we design interventions that modify them, select and do an ethical check of the ones we choose to pilot (and validate), test (and validate), and (if those work) make a scale decision, with continuous monitoring to make sure the interventions continue to contribute to the behavior we want. Collectively, that is the Intervention Design Process and the heart of this book. Doing the IDP over and over and over is what putting behavior change at the center of our work really means.

Storytime!

When I came to work at Microsoft in 2012 as its first behavioral scientist, one of the products I worked on was Bing. At the time, there was a potential insight floating around: Kids don't search in school nearly as much as you'd think they would. After all, school is supposed to encourage curiosity, so shouldn't search engines be pretty much the default tool for scratching that itch?

As with any potential insight, the first step was seeing if we were actually onto something or just chasing ephemera. The reason we call an insight "potential" is that in science we start by assuming things aren't true until we can prove they are, rather than the reverse. This healthy skepticism about assumptions is what drives rigor and why we continually validate what we think we know. So I went in search of data: I collected the IP addresses and total student populations of a few school districts, pulled query logs, then computed a daily QPS (queries per student; I was very proud of that one until I discovered the engineers already used it for queries per second) and found that it was less than one. That felt small—one query per student per day seemed unusual, given that these were tech-savvy young people with classwork to do.

But data alone does not good validation make. So I visited some classrooms to watch how kids were naturally engaging with search in the current environment. The observations jibed with the data, giving us what scientists call convergent validity: evidence that is greater than the sum of its parts because disparate sources support the same conclusion. Getting data to agree with data is all well and good, but being able to observe qualitatively what also appears to be true quantitatively is better. In this case, that meant seeing that kids were certainly on computers a lot but weren't searching much, hence the QPS (yep, still great) of less than one.

Having validated that there was an opportunity for change, I wrote a behavioral statement that described the end point we wanted to pursue: roughly "when students have a curiosity question, and they are in school and near a computer with internet connectivity, they'll use Bing to answer it (as measured by QPS)." Together with a team of people from across Bing and the wider Microsoft community, I started to map out the pressures that were encouraging or discouraging kids to search. All sorts of promoting pressures came up, everything from the social desirability of *knowing* (mmm, gnosticism . . . tasty) to the requirements of homework. And they were matched by a similar variety of inhibiting pressures,

START AT THE END

including the speed, complexity, and nonintuitive presentation of results.

And so we went back out into the classroom to validate the pressures that we had proposed. Or we were supposed to; before we could, someone in Marketing got very attached to the idea of curiosity as a promoting pressure and was hell-bent on launching immediately into a multimillion-dollar advertising campaign all about the wonder of the world. If this sounds familiar, it should—years later, Google spent a small fortune on a Super Bowl ad with this concept while trying to promote voice-assisted search (I had nothing to do with it).

The overeager marketer went so far as to make mock-ups before I managed to pump the brakes and take a group of folks back out into classrooms to watch kids. We promptly validated that second graders do *not* have a problem with curiosity. Actually, most adults wish they had fewer questions; one student asked, in rapid succession, why I didn't wear a lab coat if I was a scientist, whether I knew his uncle who worked at Microsoft, and whether he could have permission to go to the bathroom. In this case, promoting pressures didn't seem to be the problem, as there was plenty of raw curiosity to power search behavior. And a massive ad campaign to fuel what was already in ample supply was going to be a huge waste of budget (to be fair to the marketer, we have a natural bias toward promoting pressures).

What validation showed us was that the world-as-is was

being driven by the inhibiting pressures of teachers, not students: they were concerned about online safety, exposing kids to advertising, and privacy, plus trying to fit search into the curriculum in a way that allowed kids to exhaust their curiosity without sheer chaos. So we dug in to understand those pressures.

Inappropriate content was an obvious one, specifically something search engineers refer to as "adult leakage" (a subliminal plug for Depends if I've ever heard one). Teachers knew how to deal with explicitly adult searches; if little Johnny was searching for "boobs," there was a protocol for that, and not one that generally ended well for little Johnny. But it was another thing entirely when a search for "girl on a bike" generated bikini models on Harleys instead of little girls on trikes. Naughty search results weren't the students' or Bing's fault per se, but adult leakage was problematic enough (you see what I did there? Depends owes me a check) to limit search in the classroom.

Advertising was also straightforward. Search is monetized by ads, which often then follow you around the web courtesy of ad networks. Yet schools are nominally ad-free zones; brands may make small children into walking billboards on a regular basis, but teachers don't want to participate in monetizing children's searches because it is inconsistent with their identity as stewards of the classroom. And identity is the most powerful pressure I know.

The concerns about lack of privacy were a bit more nebulous. Even back then, teachers couldn't really tell us what they thought Google was doing with their students' information. But there was a general presumption that it wasn't good, and Bing was getting lumped into the same category. When it comes to promoting and inhibiting pressures, a feeling is as powerful as a fact (often more so). Though our engineers insisted that lack of privacy wasn't a technical problem, I convinced them that we needed to address teachers' feelings and proved it by suggesting the engineers call their moms and ask about search engines spying on people. Qualitative validation for the win!

Finally, there was just the practical reality that teaching kids is hard. Really hard. I taught eighth grade for a semester in order to get my teaching degree, and it was one of the most difficult things I've ever done. Teachers spend a massive amount of time on classroom management, and trying to teach search without structure felt too chaotic. They wanted their kids to be curious, but they didn't want the classroom to devolve into *Lord of the Flies*.

Having firmly squashed the multimillion-dollar curiosity ad campaign, we used the validated pressures to design interventions specifically against those four inhibiting pressures and then selected several that looked promising. We then convened people from across the organization to finalize an ethical check, as well as sitting down with an external policy think tank specializing in digital inclusion in schools to make sure we didn't have any blind spots when it came to our own interventions. And then it was finally time: we piloted with three local schools using a twofold approach of structured short search activities with daily lesson plans centered on the Bing homepage image (for those who have never been, Bing has a *National Geographic*–like photograph every day), combined with a specialized version of Bing with SafeSearch locked on to minimize leakage (yep, still fun), no search ads, and reduced data collection. As a pilot, it was unpolished, or what I like to call "operationally dirty": I wrote the first lesson plans myself, and the search experience was hacked together out of existing features with minimal new code.

And yes, the lesson plans were framed as "designed specifically to foster curiosity." Good behavioral design uses science as a process but isn't about producing pure truths, and sometimes currying favor with the marketing department isn't such a bad thing. Repeat after me: we are outcome focused, we are outcome focused, we are outcome focused. Say it until you believe it.

The pilot was easy to validate: qualitatively kids and teachers were enthusiastic, and quantitatively QPS went up—not significantly, but in the right direction. That was all the proof we needed to move on to a test, with much bigger districts, lesson plans made by a professional curriculum designer (glad we didn't blow our budget on those curiosity ads!), and the full support of Engineering to build out a robust tech solution.

As with all good tests, this was where we started to see whether the juice was worth the squeeze. It is actually fairly easy to find interventions that change behavior at least somewhat; the hard part is finding ones that are worth the effort. For example, Engineering wanted to make a desktop client that had to be installed on each machine; district computer administrators shit a brick and promised a curse on the house of Bing should that be the actual rollout mechanism.

IT is mostly about doing whatever has the lowest inhibiting pressures, because it's consistently understaffed and overworked, so I got my way and we rolled our solution out via a simple form: tell us your IP range and presto, you're enabled. For the bigger districts, I could simply fly around and convince them that this was worth prioritizing, but there were concerns about whether smaller districts would be willing to self-enroll, even with the simplified form, which was why testing was so important.

Meanwhile Marketing was trying to figure out how to get parents involved; we eventually rolled out, and then rolled back a year later, an associated Box Tops–like program where you could donate your Microsoft Rewards points to a school to provide laptops. The pilot was all right, but the test showed us it wasn't a powerful enough promoting pressure, which is why we test things. You don't have to be right all the time; you just need to make small mistakes instead of big ones.

Validation showed us it was working. Districts were getting on board, the initial press was positive, and the data was now both significant and positive: 40 percent more searches in school, plus an unexpected bonus of 15 percent more searches at home. And so we made a scale decision—Bing in the Classroom debuted with seven of the ten largest districts already committed to the platform (I think I got Alaska Airlines status for life flying around to make that happen) and seven million kids under coverage on launch day. The Analytics team continuously monitored to make sure the QPS increases were stable, and then the whole IDP kicked off again for V2.

To appreciate the magnitude of the behavior change, keep in mind that search market share was so hotly contested in those days that a tenth of a percent in movement was newsworthy. We got 40 percent more searches out of a simple product and some lesson plans, because we knew what behavior we wanted at the end and, Marketing be damned, worked backward to design the interventions to get us there. *Hasta la vista*, baby! (That quote just doesn't get enough airtime since Schwarzenegger became a governor. You're welcome.)

Indeed, the damn thing worked so well that we forced Google to do the same; within six months, it had to forgo tens of millions of ad dollars by turning off advertising in schools. Such is the nature of industries and behavior change; when you do it successfully, you remove the inhibiting pressure of doing it first, so others frequently attempt to fast-follow, though without any understanding of the validated pressures you used to create the behavior change and thus a significant handicap on their success.

There it is, Bing in the Classroom, and a happy ending if there ever was one. It took almost a year from insight to scale, but the core of the process, from insight to pilot, was about eight weeks. This is fairly typical: roughly a week to get your arms around the insight, two weeks of validation and exploration of potential pressures, a week of intervention design and selection, two weeks to get the pilots up and running, and two weeks to get back some early quantitative and qualitative signals for validation.

So now you know the IDP, at least at the highest possible level. If you are looking for a chance to stop reading, this is it. Otherwise, it is time to break it down (Hammer time!), starting with potential insights and how we validate them.

2.

POTENTIAL INSIGHTS AND INSIGHT VALIDATION

One of the central pillars of any good sci-fi mythos is the multiverse, the idea that every time a choice is made, the timeline branches and two new universes are created, one in which the choice goes one way and one in which it goes the other. Flip a coin and you get a heads universe and a tails universe, both existing side by side. Some physicists actually believe this really happens, although that would suggest there is some universe where I don't wear cowboy boots every day and that's just sad.

Theoretically, this implies that there is one universe that is nearly optimal (the Utopian Universe) and one that is almost perfectly suboptimal (the Murphy's Law Universe), with a spectrum of universes in between. I'd like to think our universe is toward the utopian end, but there is no way to truly know; optimality is hard to measure. But I am absolutely certain we do not live in the Murphy's Law Universe, the worst possible version of things, because we have Flamin' Hot Cheetos.

If physicists are right, somewhere out there are deprived universes without Flamin' Hot Cheetos. Tongues do not burn, eyes do not water, people are just less happy. All because they missed a key potential insight, so the universe bifurcated and they got the inferior version. That's all a potential insight really is: the recognition of some potential split and the opportunity to move closer to the utopian end of the spectrum. A potential insight expresses the distance between those two universes and, once validated, allows us to start understanding the gap and how to design interventions that bridge it.

With Bing in the Classroom, the insight was "Kids don't search as much as their innate, demonstrable curiosity says they would." The intervention we designed moved us from a suboptimal branch of the multiverse where kids don't search to a more optimal branch where kids do search. With

Flamin' Hot Cheetos, the potential insight was "There aren't really any Cheetos for the Latinx market."

The story of Flamin' Hot Cheetos is a fascinating one, an accidental case study in the IDP. Its protagonist is a janitor at Frito-Lay, Richard Montañez, who gets hold of some unflavored Cheetos and has the no-Latinx-Cheetos insight. So he makes what is essentially *elote* (a Mexican street food of spice-dusted corn on the cob) and starts to share his creation with his friends as an unofficial pilot. Their enthusiasm validates the insight and Montañez calls the CEO, who encourages a larger pilot. Montañez, in true pilot form, makes and bags the snacks himself to present to the CEO's team. A more formal market test leads to scaling and thus Frito-Lay's top-selling snack product. All from that one core insight: there was an alternative, more optimal version of the world in which Frito-Lay did make a product for Latinxs.

The IDP exists simply to make such alternative realities come into being, to take potential insights and run that potential to ground to see if it can create value. There are four major types of potential insights: quantitative, qualitative, apocryphal, and external.

The first is driven by, as the name implies, data. It usually comes out of either the recognition of a pattern—like an unexpected and unexplained correlation that seems to keep popping up—or the study of outliers, either positive or negative.

This is one of the reasons that simply wallowing in data is so important and why not all data wallowing should be hypothesis driven. Finding novel potential insights is about noticing something that hasn't been noticed before, and that's awfully hard to do if you're relying on existing hypotheses to guide you. You become your own worst limitation. When you let the data guide you to a potential insight, you often discover things that you feel like you've known all along (because your brain likes to feel congruent and smart) but that you would never have generated a priori.

Qualitative insights are similar but derived from subjective experience rather than carefully curated numerical tables. If you've ever been people watching and had that little tickle in your brain that says, "Hmm, that's interesting," you've had a qualitative insight. And the best way to produce those is by talking to and observing the diversity of people in the world (whether or not they already use your product; sometimes it even helps to intentionally learn about people who don't), something we all know but rarely do. Charles Pearson, one of the user researchers at Clover Health, organized volunteer trips to senior living communities for Clover employees so that they could see what it meant to be an older adult in America, and that's exactly the right strategy; you can't force insights, but you can create an environment in which they are more likely to happen. The quantitative equivalent is having an open data approach to your organization's data warehouse, another thing Clover does well: anyone at the company can learn thirty minutes of SQL and then start generating insights.

Apocryphal insights aren't directly observed; they just seem to be common knowledge in your organization. Bing in the Classroom really started here. Everyone at Microsoft just knew students weren't searching, without really being sure why they knew that. Pay attention to apocryphal insights, especially when you first come into an organization. I have an informal rule that I won't manage people the first year of a new job, and it is precisely because I want to hear what everyone thinks they already know so that I can start to validate or discard it. And when I do manage people, I pay for newbies to have lunch with colleagues from across the company and document the apocryphal insights they hear for future validation. Because once you're immersed, you just tend to accept what is believed by others as actually known and lose that outside perspective all too quickly.

Finally there are external insights. These come from beyond your organization, out in the wide world. Research papers are good for external insights, but so is simply cross-pollinating with other industries and disciplines. One of my favorite sports is taking random grad students to lunch and then just trying to figure out what everyone in their field believes to be true that might be applicable to my work. Grad students are the single most untapped resource I know of in academia. They've chosen to devote their lives to a topic, but nobody in industry ever gives them the chance to talk about it. Take a note: buy lunch for grad students. Better yet, use them as consultants who actually know something and pay them fairly for their knowledge. Because as with apocryphal insights, you need input from people other than you to really get the most out of the IDP.

No matter which kind of insight gives rise to the process, you should never simply assume truth; remember, in science everything is assumed false until proven. Particularly with apocryphal and external insights, people will speak with confidence based simply on something they heard from someone else, in some insane game of telephone that usually butchers whatever the original insight was. So once a potential insight is surfaced, it must be validated through insight validation. What we're looking for here is convergent validity: evidence from diverse sources that supports the same conclusion. For example, if we are looking at the data around prescription drugs and suspect, from looking at home and fill addresses, that people might not be going to the optimal pharmacy, we should use other sources of insight to triangulate that as a potentially valid insight. For qualitative validation, we might talk directly to members, look at call transcripts and do call listening, or ask pharmacists what they've observed. Apocryphally, we can ask knowledgeable members of our organization and see if the insight rings true for them, totally subjectively. And we can look at external research (Google Scholar is your friend) on pharmacy selection trends to see what is known beyond our organization.

Validation must be deeply embedded and constant throughout the entire IDP. Think of it like building a table—you want multiple legs, as far apart as you can get them, to hold up your conclusions. This is how we resist the *Mad Men* world, in which people build things based simply on their own personal beliefs and then manipulate data or other sources so they appear to support it (data scientists everywhere are nodding knowingly right now). Your brain, being the lazy mofo that it is, has a tendency to cheat and use something we call the confirmation bias: as soon as you start to believe something, it begins to selectively attend to evidence in order to support that belief, because changing your mind costs cognitive resources and your brain is a couch potato. The more varied your sources of convergent validity, the harder it is to fall victim to confirmation bias.

One effective way to get the legs of your table farther apart is to assign each type of validation to a different kind of researcher who specializes in each method, then cross-training them to be able to check one another. If each researcher works independently before they come back together, there is less of a tendency to cheat and proceed with an unvalidated insight or to reach group consensus too early. My team at Clover Health has both quantitative and qualitative researchers, as well as a rotating three-month fellowship for an outside master's or PhD student to do nothing but external validation (once again, grad students are your friend). Once a week the researchers and project managers come together to compare insights for convergent validity and to find potential insights generated by one discipline that the others can dig into. They also have T time.

Good behavioral scientists are T-shaped: they have one area of deep expertise (the legs of the T) and broad interests across other disciplines (the arms of the T). So on Fridays we have an hour when someone teaches a method from their legs to the rest of us for whom that isn't our core discipline, broadening our arms. And then we spend another hour meeting as functional groups, so that researchers within a discipline can go deep to expand their legs.

The reason to spend so much time on training is that this kind of cross-validation actually happens throughout the IDP, to help us avoid making large bets based on incorrect assumptions. We can never be absolutely certain about the truth behind any insight, pressure, or intervention, but by triangulating from data and observation and structurally resisting groupthink, we can eliminate risks and increase our chances of a successful, scaled outcome. This is behavioral science, and part of science is a willingness to be wrong. That's why good managers reward invalidating an insight as much as validating one.

It is also important to focus on what you are validating. Too often people use research simply as a post hoc process of confirmation bias to affirm whatever they already think they know, particularly when there are differences in organizational power between those who suggest the insights and those who are tasked with validating them. This is exaggerated in a "just ship it" culture, where the minimum viable product (MVP) takes the place of user research. The idea becomes that if you simply launch a product, people's reaction to that product is the only research you really need. But what are you truly validating? If we simply launched Flamin' Hot Cheetos and they weren't immediately popular, what should we conclude? That the Latinx market is uninteresting? That the snacks were marketed badly? That the flavor isn't right? And if they are popular, how do you launch the next version when you have no idea why the first one worked?

The point of validation is that it allows us to build toward behavior change not by popping off a silver bullet and hoping we hit the target but by a scientific process of advancement that makes sure we do. Make no mistake: the MVP culture is the product of a founder-centric, risk-taking myth that is really just about privilege and stacking the deck with high cards. Adam Grant thoroughly debunked this in *Originals* and he's hardly the only one; the focus on risk taking is a product of cognitive bias. Remember what The Streets said— validation is what makes a low straight work—and add in a little boxing wisdom: slow is smooth, smooth is fast. There is no such thing as wasted time in validation.

Town Halls and Diversity in Insight Generation

Think about our friend Richard, Knight of the Holy Cheeto. The way he turned his insight into a hugely successful (and hugely delicious) behavior change isn't exactly typical. Did you notice that I said he was a janitor? From an underrepresented minority? And that he called the CEO? That's because Frito-Lay, with over 55,000 employees, does something that very few companies in its industry do: it listens to them. In their employee onboarding training, they're encouraged to call the CEO whenever they think it is warranted (strong promoting pressure), and the CEO's direct office number is given (reduced inhibiting pressure).

Generating insights horizontally—that is, agnostic of hierarchy—throughout a company works for many reasons. With Richard, there was no formal suggestion process at all: he had an idea and, despite his job title, ran with it all the way to the top. It's a rare but exemplary instance of seeing the overlap between your consumers and your employees, and in this case it was a win-win all around; Richard is now an executive at Frito-Lay and a motivational speaker, spreading the word about the value of each person having a voice in their work.

This success wasn't just serendipity. Frito-Lay designed a system that allowed a potential insight to surface. The processes for cross-department communication and cooperation will define the throughput of potential insights that are generated in your organization. And so will the resources you devote to collection and validation. For Bing in the Classroom, I had to do both the quantitative and qualitative validation myself, which violates our separation rule and was exhausting (I cried and tried to rage-quit a lot during this period of my time at Microsoft). By allowing people to own their insights while providing them with easily accessible validation resources, you get the best of both worlds and plenty of grist for the mill that is the IDP.

That's because, in general, better intervention design happens when you have as many potential insights as possible at the beginning of the process—a big, wide funnel of opportunities for behavior change that slowly gets narrower as we hone in on pressures we're able to successfully design interventions around. The more insights we have to start with and the faster and more thoroughly we can validate them, the more interventions we can design. Designing more interventions means running more pilots, and when we thoroughly and swiftly validate those, we get more Cheeto flavors that keep bringing us closer to the Utopian Universe, one snack at a time.

I can't resist an extra example, particularly because it highlights former president and perpetual badass Barack Obama (who presided over the first White House administration to have a formal behavioral science unit). During the Obama years, he used the letter office of the White House to collect a massive number of potential insights from average Americans, which he then turned over to his staff to run down and validate. Barack Obama, behavioral scientist. See, it isn't just for janitors!

Men's clothing company Bonobos is a great example of the other reason why horizontal works—it treats people's observations and visions of counterfactual worlds with respect. If an employee with especially large calves has trouble with the fit of slim-cut pants, he isn't shamed for it and is instead encouraged to let other employees know. Steve Ballmer at Microsoft was famous for jokingly pretending to stomp on an employee's iPhone at an all-company meeting, which got some cheap laughs but sent very much the wrong message. Remember how I refuse to manage people at the beginning of my time at a company so I can keep my objectivity? Yes, we need to dogfood our own products, but we also need to respect the experience that people have with them and the legitimate other choices they might make.

Mr. Large Calves' insight is valuable, because surely another guy will have the same problem, so by responding to his insight Bonobos will be able to sell a style that appeals to more customers. The better version of the world where pants always fit, no matter what body type, is manifested. Plus, that employee feels heard, and when he goes back to his desk as a "ninja" customer service representative (yes, that's what they call them at Bonobos), he may be more apt to really hear and listen to a customer's complaint and back up the company that literally let him stretch his legs more. Good customer service makes happy customers and customers are really no different from employees. So why not use your internal resources to do the work of changing behavior for and with you?

If you're Frito-Lay, you ask your employees what flavors they want. If you're Microsoft, you make all your employees' email addresses visible and hold a monthly town hall. If you're Bonobos, you take your personalized-fit policy to the streets (or office hallways) by making your employees—men of all shapes and sizes—your fit models and getting their feedback. Here is an action you can take tomorrow: go in to work and talk to the janitor. And if you have no idea how to do that, that's half the problem.

Insight generation is inherently exciting and, like behavior change itself, inherently human. Our ability to imagine other worlds is often what makes living in this one tolerable, if not downright fun, because we can clearly see the outcome of our own potential satisfaction in vibrant Technicolor. Literally, insights start us at the end; the universe that isn't yet real gets so close you can taste it. And maybe it tastes like the kicked-up Cheetos that didn't exist until someone let their taste buds lead them down a new path to a more delicious and optimal world.

The key is to focus those insights on behaviors, not on how we create them. You have to fall in love with the problem, not the solution. Because even though we like to talk about the Cheetos, the real insight was that members of the Latinx market weren't eating Cheetos as much as they could be. We need slim-cut pants that fit guys with large calves, but there is more than one way to get there, and that's why we write a behavioral statement before we start doing intervention design. To wit, the next chapter.

3.

BEHAVIORAL STATEMENT

'm a mediocre cook. I like feeding people and always prepare way too much food, but I'm not exactly *sous vide–ing* anything. Real chefs often express a gentle, benevolent pity toward my cooking; a professional food blogger friend once congratulated me on having made excellent Thai curry. I didn't have the heart to tell him it was intended to be Indian.

But the meal wasn't a failure. Why? Because despite having intended to make Indian, "cooking good Indian food" wasn't my behavioral goal. I cook because I want to bring people together. I want them to have good conversation. I want to smile at them and I want to make them smile at one another. My real behavioral statement is about repeat eaters: I want people to come back and hang out no matter what I'm cooking. The actual food that's on the table, be it good Thai or bad Indian or anything else edible (even inedible would probably still spark conversation, just of a different kind), is irrelevant as long as it produces that outcome.

Whether an intervention succeeds or fails depends on how we define our behavioral goal. If the desired outcome was cooking Indian food, my Thai-seeming cuisine failed spectacularly. But if the goal is bringing people together, first you decide on the people you want and then, like Kevin Costner in *Field of Dreams*, you build it so they come. If we accept this book's goal—to put behavior change at the center of our creation process—then in order to be successful, we need to clearly express the behavioral outcome that we want to achieve. In other words, we have to start at the end (yes, I am going to keep saying that over and over; get used to it).

To do that, we write a behavioral statement: an articulation of the world we are trying to create, written from an explicitly behavioral perspective. This description of the counterfactual world, which we realize exists through our insights and insight validation, lays the foundation for our next steps on the IDP yellow brick road, namely pressure mapping and eventually intervention design.

Like so many things in this book, the need for an explicit goal seems obvious. But think back to Bing in the Classroom. Almost immediately, Marketing got fixated on the process, dreaming about their campaign to encourage curiosity. They lost sight of what we actually cared about as soon as they decided on an intervention that felt promising. You'll see this happen over and over again, and it is the dominant mistake of modern business.

Don't worry if this feels familiar. The tendency to focus on processes over outcomes is actually a natural psychological operation: because we spend the majority of our cognitive resources on what is happening right now—which makes sense, since we do actually have to act in order to create change—we're biased toward focusing on those immediate actions and how we're doing them, rather than on their outcomes. Means over ends, or *whats* and *hows* over *whys*. The actions are more psychologically available, while the outcomes recede into the mental distance. That's why frameworks like the IDP are so important: they help us make better, more clear-eyed choices about how to get things we want by imposing a process that fights our natural biases.

At its core, a behavioral statement is simply a set of binary conditions that can either be satisfied or not. A typical behavioral statement has five variables that come together into a single sentence:

> When [population] wants to [motivation], and they
> [limitations], they will [behavior] (as measured by
> [data]).

If the grammar of that sentence made your brain cringe a little (as it did my editor, multiple times), let's step back and define each variable so we're all speaking the same language:

Population = the group of people whose behavior you are trying to change

Motivation = the core motive for why people engage in a behavior

Limitations = the binary preconditions necessary for the behavior to happen that are outside your control

Behavior = the measurable activity you want people to always do when they have the motivation and limitations above

Data = how you quantify that they are doing the behavior

Note that each of these things can be answered with a 0 or a 1, a yes or a no. You are either in the population or not, you either want something or don't, you either meet the conditions or don't, you either do the thing or don't, and there's either evidence or there isn't.

How do behavioral statements work in the wild? Let's go with one of the clearest examples I know: Uber has done a remarkably good job of driving a very clear, direct behavioral statement, and that is a large part of why it is successful.

Quick aside: fuck Travis Kalanick. If you are an exec and you aren't actively fighting sexism in your own company, you're a sexist. And even though he isn't the CEO anymore, he still owns a large portion of the company and every Uber ride enriches him. I use the Uber example because I want a particular behavioral outcome (you apply the IDP after reading this book), and you don't always have to like an intervention for it to work. But seriously . . . fuck Travis, take a Lyft.

Uber was founded to solve the problem of getting around in San Francisco. Internet companies were flourishing, but unlike the business hub of New York City, San Francisco lacked a massive subway system and the ability to simply step out into the street and raise your hand to get a taxi. The growth of an industry drove a new, strong motivation, and thus Uber's initial behavioral statement might have looked something like this:

When people want to get from Point A to Point B, and they have a smartphone with connectivity and

an electronic form of payment and live in San Francisco, they will take an Uber (as measured by rides).

Seems simple, right? That's the advantage of a good behavioral statement: when written with care, it is easy to di-
gest, powerfully clarifying, and grammatically correct (here's
looking at you, dear copy editor). The individual conditions
carry little risk of misinterpretation, are binary, and can be
measured. But the fact that a behavioral statement is simple
in expression doesn't mean it is easy to write one. I promise
you'll spend far more time struggling with them than you
originally intended. Trust that the work is worth it; a solid
behavioral statement will get you further than almost any
other single sentence you can write.

Let's break down Uber's statement to see why it works.

POPULATION = "PEOPLE"

Uber really was an app for everyone. If a chicken
figured out how to use a smartphone, I'm pretty
sure Uber would have given that bird a ride across
the road.

This is actually fairly unusual on two fronts.
First, most products and services have an audience
for whom they are right and a much larger audience
for whom they're not, because it is hard to find a

universal motivation that allows for a universal population. Second, the general rule of thumb is that the fewer resources you have as an organization, the narrower and more specific your behavioral statement needs to be. Uber was the epitome of a go-big-or-go-home bet; it wasn't prepared to settle for just being a better version of your local cab company. So an initially very broad population worked for it (but has and will for very, very few others). For Richard Montañez, the population in his behavioral statement was Latinxs. For me, working on Bing, it was K–12 students.

MOTIVATION = "GET FROM POINT A TO POINT B"

Uber also had the benefit of an easily defined motivation with a few special characteristics. First, the desire to go from A to B was fairly general. The company's services didn't have a specific population, as noted above, but they were also broadly applicable across time and location. Certainly there were surges to deal with during rush hour and dips in activity at 3:00 a.m., but people need to go somewhere every single day of the year, rain or shine, from many Point A's to many Point B's.

Uber's need was also general in another sense: people were already habituated to using a diverse set of methods to get around. If you lived in San Francisco at the time, you were likely using a combination of cars (including taxis), trams, trains, buses, ferries, and walking. It wasn't hard to get people to adopt a new method of transit, because they were already using so many. Certainly there were habits ingrained for utility's sake—people knew the most efficient or scenic or safest ways to get around the city, depending on what mattered to them—but these habits were weak and easily disrupted, because the biggest habit was using many methods of transport.

Taken together, these were deceptively powerful advantages for Uber in its early stage. Picking the right motivation isn't often discussed but, done well, it can be incredibly helpful.

LIMITATIONS = "HAVE A SMARTPHONE WITH CONNECTIVITY AND AN ELECTRONIC FORM OF PAYMENT AND LIVE IN SAN FRANCISCO"

This was actually the most daunting part of Uber's behavioral statement. In 2009, cell phone ownership wasn't ubiquitous, cellular service wasn't a given, and people weren't as used to storing credit card information in an app. Hell, 15 percent of the U.S. adult population didn't even have a form of electronic payment in 2009.[4]

But as a startup, Uber didn't need everyone to make it work. It just needed to demonstrate a viable enough model to attract the next round of funding, and a young, tech-centric city like San Francisco was exactly right.

Although all of a behavioral statement's variables are binary, it's especially worth noting that limitations don't exist on a scale: they're either yes or no, 1 or 0. Someone does or doesn't have a smartphone, does or doesn't have an electronic form of payment, and does or doesn't live in San Francisco and these factors are explicitly outside the company's control. This is important because it is easy to accidentally list inhibiting pressures as limitations. Being able to afford an Uber, for example, is really about expense, and perceptions of expense are variable: they can be strengthened or weakened by interventions.

It is also important to be careful not to include limitations that you intend to modify through behavior change. Because while having the Uber app is a precondition for using Uber, it isn't a limitation because it is Uber's job to make that happen, whereas Uber wasn't relocating users to San Francisco or giving them cell phones or credit cards; limitations exist precisely because we are explicitly choosing not to target interventions at them.

BEHAVIOR/DATA = "TAKE AN UBER"/"RIDES"

This is where Uber really nailed it: they knew exactly what they needed to get people to do (take an Uber) and exactly how to measure it (rides), with the added bonus that their data was generated by the product itself and didn't have to be separately gathered. Certainly there were all sorts of other metrics, like sign-ups and app opens and all the other things that get tracked inside a company, but the behavioral goal itself was automatically measured, data-complete, and nearly immediate.

As you start creating your own behavioral statements, you'll realize just how incredibly rare that is. Take Flamin' Hot Cheetos: retail sales measurement is actually an entire industry in itself, because it is very hard to track things like precisely how many bags of Cheetos have actually been sold on a moment to moment basis. I will be paid for writing this book based on the total number of books sold, but finding and verifying that number is next to impossible in any timely sort of way, because books have to be shipped out to stores and then shipped back if they don't sell, and then you have to factor in returns by people who don't like the cursing. This is one of the reasons the internet has prospered: it generates data as it goes, creating feedback loops for behavior change.

Common Mistakes in Behavioral Statements

Hopefully, the Uber example emphasizes the simplicity of a behavioral statement. But as I mentioned earlier, don't fall for the conjunction fallacy of "simple" being misread as "easy." Writing a good behavioral statement is hard, one of the hardest parts of the IDP, and there are a couple of common pitfalls you have to avoid to do it well. So let's spend a few minutes on those before moving on to pressures.

Choosing the Wrong Behavior

Easily the most common mistake is not being thoughtful enough about the actual behavior you want to change. This often comes because you're focusing on sounding good instead of being good, trying to write a vision statement instead of a behavioral one. For example, for many years the Microsoft vision statement was "A computer on every desk and in every home running Microsoft software." And while I love that vision and the great good it created (and still creates) in the world, it is a singularly bad behavioral statement.

Why? Because the mere existence of a computer isn't actually a behavior, or if it is, it is only the limited action of a one-time purchase. To really see the problem, imagine a world where the vision statement is literally true: every home and office has a computer running Microsoft software. Now envision them all unplugged, covered in a healthy layer of dust and sprinkled with last week's laundry, because nobody actually wants to use them. Nothing about Microsoft's statement is incompatible with that hypothetical reality, because the statement is about the existence of an object in a certain location and nothing more. It fails to address the *actions* implied in the vision statement coming true—those measurable behaviors that we know and love.

You might laugh at this example, but it is actually a real one that led Microsoft significantly astray. For years, the

Office product and tech teams were oriented toward sales as the metric that mattered. Accordingly, they focused on features that no home consumers cared about but that appealed to niche corporate clients. And so they introduced endless features focused on expanding the reach of the software into increasingly niche populations, making Excel the powerhouse behind modern financial analysis by creating a deep macro system and Word an essential part of the publishing industry by creating sophisticated markup languages. Don't know what those features are? There is a reason for that—they probably weren't built for you, but rather to sell an extra few licenses to some corporate customer.

Hell, the salespeople were even paid commissions on the number of licenses they sold to enterprise customers. Because remember, if we want every single computer running Microsoft software, workplaces are the primary buyers of computers and so by orienting everyone toward sales, Microsoft could bring its vision to life.

The problem was that when contract-renewal time came, CTOs were constantly trying to trim down the contracts because they had discovered that nobody in their organizations was actually using the software! The reason Google Docs came into being was that Microsoft wasn't paying attention to the actual experience of using its software—the behavior it should have been monitoring. And when it did, pivoting internally from a sales metric to a usage metric (even for the sales team!), it created Office 365 and the ribbon bar, which made Excel and Word reasonable for those of us who aren't in finance or publishing.

My editor hates me, but I can't resist another Microsoft example (also, as noted earlier, this is not saying Microsoft is bad; I own a lot of stock and enjoyed working there). Go back to the original vision statement: a computer on every desk. How do you make that happen? Drive the price of buying a computer as low as you can. Which Microsoft did, with Intel, by introducing the netbook—a low-power form factor that emphasized a no-frills approach to computing. And just as with selling Office licenses, it "worked"—in 2008, shortly after netbooks were introduced, laptop sales exceeded desktop sales for the first time.

The problem was that the average netbook in 2007 was about as powerful as a good laptop from 2001 (although admittedly at a fraction of the cost). Good for ownership, bad for usage. Because on a cheap, underpowered machine, even the best Windows experience becomes a unique kind of torture, posing a huge brand challenge—people associated the reduced experience with the operating system rather than with the machine, because most people had no idea they were buying an underpowered machine. Windows Vista, introduced around the same time, was so hated by virtually everyone that most people still shudder at the name. And Microsoft had to delay introducing richer experiences like those offered by Windows 8 and Windows 10 because it had to support a hundred million people with terrible computers.

By focusing on PC and software sales, Microsoft neglected the behavior that is computing itself. Contrast this with Apple, which never sold a computer that didn't come with an explicitly compatible operating system—this meant there was no potential confusion over whether the hardware or the software was to blame for anything less than a great experience. There's never any worry that a new MacBook or iPhone model will crash under the weight of its accompanying OS, because Apple focused on usage from the start.

Just as it had with Office, Microsoft eventually caught on. It introduced its Surface line so that, like Apple, it could show that Windows worked just fine when you made a computer powerful enough to run it well. And moves like these are what drove a 5x increase in the stock price while I was at the company; the focus on usage started to permeate the culture. Thus the renewed Microsoft of Satya Nadella that you know today. The company picked a better behavior and was rewarded for it.

Choosing No Behavior

Potentially worse than picking the wrong behavior is picking no behavior at all, and that's the second-most-common mistake. It also tends to happen when people focus on vision

START AT THE END

statements over behavioral ones and typically comes from marketing- or product-focused CEOs, often in the form of something insanely trite like "Our job is to make the customers love our product."

What the fuck does that mean?

Love isn't a behavior. You can't physically observe it and thus you can't measure it, so if you try to design for it, you will inevitably end up in the same boat as 2000s-era Microsoft. Customer love is just another post hoc rationalization for Mad Men to spend money on something they love.

And because there is no way to measure customer love, there is no way to prove that any particular intervention actually makes a customer love your product. Which means that there is no way to compare interventions against one another, short-circuiting the whole IDP. Your marketing team will spend millions and justify it with customer love and at the same time your product, tech, sales, and other teams will be running in opposite directions with precisely the same justification. A statement without a behavior is a North Star you can't navigate by.

Timid Behavioral Statements

As you've no doubt detected by this point in the book, I'm a fairly . . . *strident* person. Call that a personality flaw if you will, but when it comes to writing a behavioral statement, it is actually an important feature of success.

Uber's behavioral statement described a world in which people would always use Uber when they needed to go from Point A to Point B, not sometimes but *always*. As is true of other things in Uber's history, that's a ballsy statement. There are so many modes of transportation these days, and cars in general aren't always the best option; there's traffic, greenhouse gas emissions, potential parking fees, stolen tires, etc. All those limiting pressures are the reasons people don't already choose a car all the time. So why describe the absolute?

Because it increases the likelihood you'll get there. A typical process-based design system asks: "If we are here, how are we going to move the ball down the field, closer to the goal?" I want you to ask: "In the perfect world the ball is already downfield *in the goal* and we have won the game. What play do we need to run to cause that to be true?" These two statements sort of sound the same because they both see the current world and desired world on opposite ends of the playing field and both try to get us from here to there. But this is where one of those pesky mental heuristics gets in the way: anchoring and adjustment.

Answer this question quickly: how tall is the Statue of Liberty, taller or shorter than ten feet? Obviously taller, but how much taller? For the sake of time—and since I can't hear your answer—let's say you guess a hundred feet.

Now I'll ask someone else the same question but phrase it like this: how tall is the Statue of Liberty, taller or shorter than a thousand feet? You might say shorter, by as much as half—so five hundred feet. Now compare the two equally valid guesses. There's a big difference between a hundred feet and five hundred feet, and it comes from the anchor that I set in the question itself. Where I place the anchor—ten or a thousand feet—changes your perception.*

Your anchor inevitably affects the interventions you design to reach it. If Apple designed an iPod based on the usage of the Discman and its finite storage capacity, it would have evolved music-listening behavior rather than fundamentally shifting us to a more optimal universe. Uber didn't base its product on gaining a beachhead in car service; it aimed for and achieved an entirely different mode of behavior. So when writing your behavioral statement, don't equivocate.

---

* To save you from Googling it, the Statue of Liberty actually measures 305 feet. You're welcome. "How Tall Is the Statue of Liberty?" 2009, www.howtallisthestatueofliberty.org.

Clinging to Your First Behavioral Statement

The last mistake is a bit more subtle: refusing to evolve a behavioral statement. Because sometimes market forces shift and you have to pivot the behavior that your company is trying to create. And even with the most audacious goal, you sometimes actually accomplish it and need to broaden.

Take Uber. You'll notice I used the past tense as I walked through its behavioral statement. That's because that statement has changed significantly since its inception and will continue to as the company evolves. That's not unusual, especially for companies that are relatively new; iteration and scale both generally allow you to broaden your behavioral statement considerably.

At the time I'm writing this, the Uber behavioral statement might sound something like this:

> When people want to get something from Point A to Point B, and they have a device with connectivity and live in a metro area in most countries, they will use an Uber (as measured by rides).

There are some big changes in there to unpack. The first, and arguably most important, is that Uber has expanded from a local transit company to a logistics company. It became so successful at acquiring drivers that it couldn't create enough demand, spread out over enough time, to fill their available drivable hours. So it started delivering more than people: take-out, groceries, and anything else that needs door-to-door transportation, thus expanding the motivation from moving just *people* to moving *anything*.

That's huge. It opens up entirely new markets, allows the company to guarantee greater revenue to drivers by smoothing out the demand curve, and creates the potential for very different forms of partnership with other large enterprises. And it also makes Uber more resilient; if people go fewer places physically because of changes in pressures beyond Uber's control, that will hurt the company's bottom line. But if they're not going places, people will likely need more things brought *to* them. Because Uber can now meet that need, it is better prepared to weather macrobehavioral shifts.

And it's indeed possible that a behavioral statement changes because of external shifts, rather than an internal shift like the growth of your product. People used to buy watches so they could know what time it was. Then cell phones were born and suddenly everyone knew the time all the time. Yet watches haven't disappeared off the face of the earth or the wrists of people. Because when the watch companies saw everyone pulling out their phones to meet the need that their product once met, they evolved their behavioral statement and found a new need watches could fill:

status. Today you see people wearing watches less to tell the time than as a way to display something about themselves. Timex-ers send a message that they value clarity and economy and nostalgia; Rolex-ers tell the world all about their black cards and black cars.

There were other changes for Uber as well. Remember how I said limitations should be binary and outside your control? Since Uber didn't want to get into the business of providing electronic banking to the world, when it moved out of just the San Francisco market, it had to remove the mobile payments limitation. So in some markets, like the Ukraine, you can pay for an Uber with cash.

Refusing to evolve your behavioral statement means that you can't go some places and do some things, and at a certain level of growth, that's not tenable. I know these statements are hard to write, but we can't get attached to them. Just as we fall in love with the behaviors we want to create rather than the interventions that create them, we must be willing to pivot when it is time.

Behavioral Statements in Planning

I promise we'll move on to pressures, and if you're truly bored, you can skip this section. But now that you know how to write a good behavioral statement, I can't resist giving you

some ideas for how to make it valuable inside your organization.

First—and hopefully this is obvious—you have to be
transparent. Put it up on the wall where everyone can see it,
mention it at every town hall, orient your planning process
toward it. The whole point of a good behavioral statement is
that it can allow for strong decision making because you can
explicitly compare available options against the behaviors
they are likely to produce. Yes, the statement may change,
but only as your business evolves in epochs, and those are
fundamental shifts you'll want to communicate broadly anyway. Paint is cheap; write it on your walls.

Second, while you should have only one behavioral statement for your organization as a whole, you can scale them
endlessly down as needed and I actually encourage it. Ultimately, the organization's behavioral statement is the thing
the CEO is held accountable for: moving (or not moving)
that behavior should be the metric by which we reward and
punish that single person at the top. But by writing smaller
behavioral statements throughout your organization, you can
help everyone find the zone within which they have autonomy and thus accountability.

Again, for consistency, let's use Uber. Imagine that the
head of the marketing department looked at the overall company behavioral statement and decided that account creation
is the largest sub-behavior they were willing to solely own.

They could write their own behavioral statement for that be-havior and be held accountable for achieving it. And that could keep going: a marketing manager for a particular re-gion could write a statement with a more specific population and be held accountable for it. And on and on to the lowliest intern, who gets "When African American women between twenty and thirty who live in Los Angeles want to get some-thing to go from Point A to Point B, and they have a device with connectivity, they will create an Uber account (mea-sured by account creation)."

The beauty of this process is twofold. First, there is a clear and direct line between what each individual person is ac-countable for and the behavioral goal of the entire organiza-tion; everyone knows why what they do matters and has an autonomous zone that they can entirely own. Second, it cre-ates clear hierarchies to that accountability. A leader is simply someone who is accountable for the larger behavioral state-ment that encapsulates those below it. No more dickering about titles and who is Chief of something and who isn't. Status is a result only of behavioral accountability.

So how do you find the right size of behavioral statement for someone at the organization? Again, it comes back to au-tonomy and accountability. The behavioral statement should be as large as possible but small enough that the person could be held individually accountable for its success or failure. For example, if we use account creation and marketing, the CMO should be willing to bet their job on that behavior statement and have enough autonomy that holding them accountable is fair.

For those who do a lot of planning, notice the similarity between a behavioral statement and an objective and key result (OKR). "As measured by data" is really just the *KR* and the rest is just the *O*, but phrased in such a way as to be observably descriptive of the world you're trying to create. If you're already doing OKRs for your planning process, you're already ready to simply sub in behavioral statements and reorient entirely toward behavior.

All right, enough. Someone else can write a whole book about how you can use the IDP to design the interior structure of companies and to do planning; I'll simply end by noting that behavioral statements are designed to cause your organization to behave in a particular way and that organizational structure is an intervention to that same end, just like any other. Onward!

4.

PRESSURE MAPPING AND PRESSURE VALIDATION

At the highest level, behavior change is about interventions that move us from Point A (the world as it is) to Point B (the world as we want it to be). And if our insights describe Point A and our behavioral statement describes point B, what remains is to understand why Point A isn't already Point B. That is, we need to map the pressures that create the distance between what we have and what we want, so we know what it is we need to change. And that's really the secret sauce of this whole book, because when we talk about designing for behavior change, we are actually talking about changing the pressures that determine the behavior, rather than directly changing the behavior itself.

Let me illustrate and brag about my kid at the same time. While I was writing this book, I was also trying to be a good dad to a little boy named Bear, to whom this book is dedicated. Caring for an infant is a large responsibility, in part because it is one of the rare times in life when we directly control someone else's behavior, for better or worse. When he was three months old, I could fully determine most of Bear's behaviors. For example, I chose his outfit for the day and physically put him in it; he could make it easier or harder by struggling, but ultimately what I chose was what he wore.

But even in the early stages of parenthood, it's impossible to *totally* control another person's behavior. There were plenty of infant Bear's behaviors that I couldn't control, like sleeping. I could change the probability of Bear's sleep by controlling the pressures that acted on it—tiring him out (increasing the promoting pressure of sleepiness) or putting up blackout curtains (reducing the inhibiting pressure of bright light)—but I couldn't actually *make* him sleep. Without direct control, all I could do was change the pressures on both sides of the equation to maximize the likelihood of the behavior I wanted.

And that's where mapping the competing pressures that create behavior becomes crucial. Before long, Bear will choose his own clothes and I, like generations of parents before me, will have to learn how to affect the pressures that change his behavior. Because that is really all I can do for his remaining lifetime of clothing choices: give him encouragement when he chooses to wear pants without holes in them (increasing the promoting pressure for good pants) and refuse to buy him acid-washed jeans (increasing the inhibiting pressure for bad pants). I can't actually stop him from buying holey, bleached jeans himself and wearing them around town but when I design the pressures with intent, I can change the likelihood of getting the behavior I want.

Like all examples, Bear is imperfect (don't tell his mother I said that). I talked about his individual behavior, and yet usually behavior change isn't about a specific person but rather about changing the likelihood of a behavior across a much larger group: team, organization, city, nation—as we said in the behavioral statement, a population. And not any individual moment of behavior, but behavior stretched across time. So not Bear's afternoon feeding on October 14 but Bear-age children's feeding generally and for the foreseeable future.

That means that behavior change itself will be inherently imperfect. You can lose the battle—a person, a specific moment, a single unit of behavior—and still win the war. This is true because populations are, in the aggregate, largely predictable. Even if any given person might not do what we expect all the time, the overall behavior of large numbers of people across large numbers of moments is relatively normalized because we're all affected by broad pressures like cost, availability, and popularity.

So how do we start to get our arms around these pressures that underlie our predictability? People can make, and have made, lovely complex diagrams and systems that attempt to fully describe the beautiful intricacy of being human. But I'm going to stick with a diagram that even three-year-old Bear could draw:

Mind-bending, I know. But remember the goal of this book: I want you to actually create behavior change, every single day. And sometimes simple frameworks are the best way to get that done.

These arrows represent the balance of competing pressures that create our behavior: promoting pressures—the up arrow—make a behavior more likely and inhibiting pressures—the down arrow—make a behavior less likely. What we actually do is determined by the net product of those forces. If the promoting pressures overcome the inhibiting pressures, we act. If the inhibiting pressures are stronger, we don't. And both sides are equally responsible for the ultimate behavior: we can never say people don't act because of a lack of promoting pressure, because it could equally well be phrased that the overwhelming inhibiting pressures are responsible.

Picture one of those big Mylar balloons you got for your birthday as a kid. It's full of helium and suspended in front of you, hovering in what we'll call an inactive state. The promoting and inhibiting pressures are balanced, so nothing is really happening at Point A, the current state of the world.

Now the balloon, as every storybook will tell you, really just wants to float up and up and up into the sky and fulfill its balloon destiny—that's its happy ending, its Point B, its desired behavioral end state. If you give it a little bump from below (an additional promoting pressure), you disturb the equilibrium and overwhelm existing inhibiting pressures like gravity, causing a behavior change. If you wanted to make liftoff even more likely, you could add a wind machine underneath or a little more helium inside.

But what if it were raining so hard that the balloon couldn't rise? Or what if, while you tried to push it upward, I pushed down against you? To get the balloon moving up against those downward forces—the inhibiting pressures—you'd have to push much harder, maybe add a little propeller. Or you'd have to find a way to reduce the inhibiting pressures, by blocking the rain or pushing me out of the way or, if you were really ambitious, reducing the force of gravity itself.

That is actually what we are trying to do by mapping the pressures. By understanding the rain and my pushing down

and your pushing up and gravity and all the rest, we are laying the groundwork for creating the interventions that effectively change that behavior to get us to the world we want.
We can't start adding or removing pressures until we understand, at least broadly, what exists now.

Why We Eat M&M's: Exploring Promoting Pressures

The competing pressures arrow diagram isn't an abstract representation to help you learn the concept—it is the actual
tool you're going to be using. When you start to do the IDP
for yourself, you'll go find a whiteboard or notebook or tab-
let, draw the up and down arrows, and start listing pressures
on each side. If you feel like practicing now would help, you
can draw your own diagram and fill it in as we go. Or just
imagine me doing it illegibly on a whiteboard, since we want
to keep this true to life.

Let me walk you through my favorite illustration of competing pressures: M&M's. Start with our up arrow. Why do
we eat M&M's? The easy answer is that they taste good.
Taste is a powerful promoting pressure, which is why Mars
has spent millions of dollars coming up with different M&M
flavors, more than forty so far (including the very unchoco-
late chili nut). This is clearly foolish, as we all know that

peanut butter M&M's are the pinnacle to which all other M&M's aspire. Yet Mars keeps gleefully pumping out flavors, simply because taste is clearly the main reason to eat M&M's or any other candy.

Yet it isn't taste alone that has sold billions of M&M's. M&M's are beautiful. We have a basic attraction to foods that look good, and we are preprogrammed to love that array of strong primary colors (you can blame your addiction on an evolutionary preference for brightly colored fruits and vegetables). People will eat more M&M's from a bowl that contains more colors,[5] and in 1995, when Mars dropped the least vibrant of its palette (tan—you know, the poop-colored one), more than ten million people called in to vote for its replacement (blue!).

Color may seem like a silly reason to eat M&M's, and few people would call it out as important. Yet part of getting good at pressure mapping is recognizing that there is much more at play than what people consciously identify as affecting their behavior. That's why we need insights and validations and why we'll eventually run pilots; humans have very poor introspection into our own motivations. After all, you are theoretically a very logical grown-up who reads nonfiction books like this one for pleasure. Yet you still have a favorite color of M&M, despite knowing that there is no actual difference in taste among different colors. When you were a kid, you probably ate them in a specific color order (and maybe you still do). Why? Color is strongly tied to our sense of identity. "What's your favorite color?" is one of the worst meet-and-greet questions out there, but people still love to answer it because we can shape our whole lives—wardrobe, accessories, walls, stationery—to reflect that quality that makes us a special snowflake. Color is a predictable, albeit illogical, promoting pressure for many behaviors, including eating M&M's, yet virtually no one ever names it.

Are you still so logical and grown up that you doubt color is actually important? One behavioral science trick that always helps with pressure mapping is flipping the scenario on its head and taking it to the extreme—imagining if the opposite conditions were true and thinking about how that would influence the behavior. Because a successful intervention is about creating a world that doesn't currently exist, you'll always need to be working through thought experiments and inhabiting imaginary realms. And sometimes those are worlds we explicitly *don't* want, so that we can more clearly see the world we do. Imagine if M&M's came in a shade of puke green. Or maybe piss yellow. Still think people would be so quick to shake the entire contents of a bag into their hand and toss them back like a human Pez dispenser (a candy I cannot come up with a promoting pressure for besides the dumb dispenser)?

Other times, what guides behavior is not seemingly irrational pressures like color but a kissing cousin I'm going to call counterrational pressures: pressures that are likely to be identified but viewed as promoting rather than inhibiting, or vice versa. Calories are in this category for M&M's. If I ask an audience whether calories make people more or less likely to eat M&M's, everyone always says less. They're half wrong. Fear of getting fat is an inhibiting pressure and calories are an important part of that fear. But calories themselves can also be a promoting pressure.

That seems to fly in the face of our intuition and yet it is markedly true. When does snack food consumption peak? Midafternoon. People eat lunch (increasingly featuring foods with a high glycemic index) and their blood sugar goes up, then crashes as the insulin released overwhelms the short-acting sugars. Snacking for calories is a biological imperative, and when you phrase calories as "hunger," it is a strong promoting pressure.

And some brands know this. Consider Snickers. It never runs ads that say "Snickers: We taste better than M&M's," and it's certainly not trying to compete on color (thank you, *Caddyshack*). Instead it's embraced the caloric content of its bars, from the 1980s' "Snickers really satisfies" to the more recent "Peanuts for power" to the 2010 Super Bowl commercial that cast a lagging football player as Betty White until he was transformed back into himself by a bite of chocolate and caramel, explaining, "You're not you when you're hungry." Consistently for over forty years, Snickers has advertised that when you want to be powerful, energized, and more virile than a ninety-year-old woman (no offense to Betty), you eat a Snickers.

Again, the trick to getting good at pressure mapping is learning to let go of your natural assumptions, to see the irrational and the counterrational as opportunities. It is also recognizing that there are diminishing marginal returns: no behavior can ever be fully pressure mapped, so knowing when enough is enough depends on the maturity of the market. Some categories have been around so long that focusing on the disruptive, unrecognized pressures is key; others are so new that just getting the most obvious pressures right is enough to produce real change.

The list of promoting pressures really could go on endlessly. M&M's have strong positive cultural associations: they're iconic, nostalgic, and distinctively American (indeed, the official candy of the White House). The brand is synonymous with lighthearted fun, as narrated by giant animated candies, an image Mars has spent hundreds of millions to create and maintain. They're also ubiquitous—a regular option in the school or office vending machine that feels familiar and comfortable. Again, we wouldn't eat M&M's because of branding or ubiquity alone if they tasted or looked terrible, but given that they're delicious, all of the extra cultural connotations certainly help drive consumption.

Why We Don't Eat M&M's:
Exploring Inhibiting Pressures

So we now know that M&M's are delicious, beautiful, full of hunger-fighting calories, and coated with good feelings. You nodded along faithfully to all my previous paragraphs, like good readers, and are now entirely convinced about the many reasons we want to eat them.

And yet you aren't eating them right now.

Boom! Talk about a counterfactual universe. You just agreed with that laundry list of promoting pressures and yet you live in a world where you're not actually eating M&M's most of the time. Clearly, I'm a quack and this book should be immediately returned or burned or whatever it is we're doing with heresy these days.

To be fair, you should have seen this coming. There were two arrows and "Why do we eat M&M's?" is only one of our two key questions. Life isn't just a giant soup of unchecked motivations; there are always inhibiting pressures that make any particular behavior less likely. So if our behavioral statement is one of eating M&M's all the time, we need to also consider why we aren't already doing that.

So why aren't you eating M&Ms right now? This is where my degree in mind reading psychology comes in handy. The reason you're not is that you're not sitting next to a giant bowl of M&M's. How do I know? Because if you were, I can say with a high degree of certainty that you would be eating them. Physical availability is one of the key inhibiting pressures to M&M consumption and pretty much everything else in life; humans are remarkably attuned to proximity.

We all know this intuitively. Think about a bowl of candy on your desk versus one across the room; you don't have to do the thought experiment, you just intuitively know how quickly you would mindlessly eat through the close one while the far one went untouched. All pressures exist along a spectrum. Availability isn't black and white, and by adjusting the strength of the inhibiting pressure that is availability—that is, by putting M&M's in your cabinet or on a desk ten feet away, across the office, on another floor, or at the bodega around the corner—I can change the resulting behavior by corresponding degrees.

And we can do this by ramping up or down all sorts of inhibiting pressures. Physical availability is one factor, but so is psychological availability. In one office-based study, workers consumed an extra two chocolates per day when the candy was on their desk versus across the room, but they consumed two *more* when the bowl was clear versus opaque.[6] "Out of sight, out of mind" holds true after all. Google is famous for doing this at scale; it put all the office candy in opaque containers but kept the fruits and nuts in clear ones.

Over seven weeks, employees ate a cumulative 3.1 million fewer calories.[7]

There are also counterrational pressures at play on the inhibiting side, like whether or not branding fits a context. Lighthearted and fun is great for kids, but picture a romantic Valentine's Day dinner. Candlelight, filet mignon, roses, red wine, and for dessert . . . *M&M's*. It just doesn't work. That's a Lindt moment, a Ferrero Rocher moment, a foil-wrapped, liqueur-infused, dark chocolate moment. The same branding that makes M&M consumption more likely in one context makes it less likely in another.

Calories are another example: promoting pressure in the form of blood sugar in the midafternoon, inhibiting pressure in the form of health concerns when I get out of the shower and am confronted with the dad bod. That's why we have to be specific in a behavioral statement about not only the behavior we want but also the population and context in which we want it.

All pressures interact with context, in terms of changing both their strength and even, in extreme cases, their direction. Take the strength of cost as an inhibiting pressure: a dollar may not seem like much, but watch a five-year-old save their allowance to buy a bag of M&M's, or grapple with the fact that most of the world lives on less than $2.50 a day, and you may change your opinion about just how inhibiting a dollar really is. Or enjoy the counterrational pressure of higher prices making people more likely to buy something because a high price communicates either quality or luxury, two strong promoting pressures. Even color is not immune, when bright color equals artificial equals unhealthy. Just ask the Brits: the M&M equivalent in the UK is Smarties, which went noticeably more pastel when the maker started using natural food dyes.

As with promoting pressures, I could spend an entire book on the Encyclopedia of Inhibiting Pressures and not even scratch the surface. It wouldn't be a useful manual, however, because ultimately all pressures are context dependent; they interact with motivation, population, and one another in unique ways. This is why the IDP features so much validation and emphasizes the pilot/test/scale motion: the only way to know you've identified the right pressures is to use them to build interventions that actually change behavior.

Avoid Predictable Problems

What is more important than the specific pressures is considering both sides of the equation. Because it turns out, to borrow a turn of phrase from Dan Ariely, humans are predictably irrational. In a series of experiments in my lab, we showed that when asked to focus on creating *more* of a behavior, people almost exclusively generated interventions aimed at increasing promoting pressures, like rewards. When focused on creating *less* of a behavior, they disproportionately generated interventions ramping up inhibiting pressures, like punishments.

Hence the world as it exists today. We all intuitively get the behavior-changing power of the candy bowl that moves from desk to bookcase to kitchen to bodega, yet what would we actually create if Mars hired us? The forty-second flavor of M&M. We logically understand the power of reducing inhibiting pressures by moving M&M's closer to people but still focus on making them more attractive.

But don't despair. This predictable error means that there is also predictable untapped upside. For Uber it was reducing inhibiting pressures. As it started in the black car space, all of its competitors were focused on promoting pressures. It won't be a black car, it will be a silver Audi with a minibar and a disco ball synced to your playlist, driven by Claudia Schiffer and powered by the defensive line of the Raiders!

What Uber recognized is that the desire to go from Point A to Point B is sufficiently strong that the majority of the task is just reducing inhibiting pressures and Uber's product and marketing are in lockstep on this framing. Sure, every once in a while it does a promotion like "Today the ride comes with puppies" or ice cream bars or flu shots, or it will be a Tesla. But what are the three emails you regularly get from

Uber? "It is now cheaper than it was before" (lowered inhibiting cost), "There are now more drivers on the road" (lowered inhibiting wait time), and "We can now go somewhere we couldn't before" (lowered inhibiting range). Uber's entire business is based on reducing inhibiting pressure.

Indeed, one could argue that Uber's strongest behavior-changing feature is automatic payment. Paying for a cab is a strong inhibiting pressure. The physical loss of money that marks a cash transaction is highly salient, such that even small children would rather pay with a credit card than cash to avoid that feeling of loss.[8] In some ways, I'm disappointed that Uber was invented in San Francisco; if you've ever been in the East Village in New York City on a one-way street on a Friday, frantically trying to get the card reader to accept your credit card while a thousand cabs behind you lay on their horns, you have a sense of just how painful the process of payment, not even the cost, actually is. And yet until Uber made automatically paying for transport ubiquitous, few would have been able to articulate the power of eliminating this common experience, because we would have been so focused on the promoting pressures.

Both promoting and inhibiting pressures can be used to change any behavior, which is why we draw the arrows and populate both sides to overcome our biases. Imagine if someone at Mars reads this book and does precisely that, ignoring their natural tendency to create the forty-second flavor and focusing on inhibiting pressures. If they take the same multimillion-dollar budget for product development and food safety and marketing and voting for a new bag color and instead challenge their workforce with a simple directive—make M&M's available everywhere, all the time—then we all will have to start worrying about dad bod. Auto-refill dispensers, distribution deals, snack subscription services—suddenly a massive new list of potential interventions becomes the focus.

Once you've drawn the arrows and successfully avoided bias, where do all these pressures come from? In the *Mad Men* world you just make them up to justify the interventions you want to run. But in the IDP we generate them in the same way we generated insights: research and convergent validity. Fortunately, all of the interviews and data science you did in search of insights also naturally lend themselves to the mapping and validating of pressures. So when you get in a room and draw the arrows and start to fill in the pressures, you can prevent a *Mad Men* world simply by sticking to the work you've already done. And if new pressures are revealed, you just go validate them, because your research team is in the room for the pressure mapping and intervention design; they are the closest to what can be known from existing work and they will be the ones to validate before moving on, so you want them there as the potential pressures are generated.

There are other things you can do to help make sure you get as complete a pressure map as possible. Focus on just inhibiting or promoting pressures and then switch. Try reversing the polarity of your behavioral statement; if you think about how to make sure no one ever takes an Uber, you'll likely uncover some pressures you can use to make sure they do. And make sure you have a diverse room. The more gender, ethnic, cultural, cognitive, and other variation you can introduce, the smaller your blind spots and the less likely you'll fall victim to biases.

Because in trying to avoid our biases and understand a rich set of pressures that act on people, we can bring it full circle (watch this, you're going to love it). In reality, *the arrows and this chapter and the whole notion of pressures is just another intervention designed to change our behavior*, to help us move away from the default of looking only at one side or the other, of making up pressures that don't validate, of seeking interventions that sell well to executives but don't change behavior. We want to create behaviors (because I ramped up the promoting pressures with the intro) and now we're overriding the natural tendencies that make it less likely that we do that (by adding processes to remove inhibiting pressures). But it works only if we successfully bridge those validated pressures with the interventions they give rise to. We need to put the ID in the IDP and make those pressures useful.

5.

INTERVENTION DESIGN AND INTERVENTION SELECTION

One of the best teachers I ever had bore a strong physical resemblance to a gnome. Even as a sixth grader, I towered over Ms. Liupakka, whose passion for math was exceeded only by her passion for mischief. She had a whip on the wall of her classroom with a sign about discipline and once, on a random Tuesday, she brought it into my art class along with a handkerchief soaked in ketchup. She called me out into the hall, smacked a ruler against the wall, and then told me to holler, just to scare the hell out of the other kids. She was a complete and total badass and I remain in awe of her more than twenty-five years later.

The only thing more memorable than that whip was a lesson she taught about creativity in our algebra class. On the overhead projector (remember those?) she put up a slide with an assortment of numbers, letters, and symbols and told us to find different ways of putting them in groups. Our young, nimble minds suggested letters versus numbers, odds versus evens, all the standard groupings that are dutifully taught as part of the subtle cultural education we all receive. But once we exhausted our imaginations, Ms. Liupakka began to suggest other patterns. Characters that appeared on a telephone versus those that didn't. Characters made of lines (*A*'s and *F*'s) versus those made of curves (*C*'s and *O*'s). She was teaching us that the goal isn't just having the most ideas; it is having *different* ideas. Better ones. Twenty-five little lightbulbs went on and we were set out into the world to become creative, status-quo-changing thinkers.

That definition of creativity—generating novel alternatives that others don't—is just as exciting to psychologists as it is to sixth graders. That which is different is intrinsically interesting and we naturally gravitate toward the unusual. And that natural bias is how all those Mad Men screwed us. I love Ms. Liupakka, and she'd wash my mouth out for saying this, but *fuck creativity*.

When we focus on novelty, we lose sight of behavioral outcomes. And while using validated pressures to inform our designs can help guard against the natural tendency to pursue interventions that feel unique, they aren't a guarantee; just as data can be used to justify bad business decisions, pressures can be used to justify bad interventions. It is entirely possible to diligently get this far into the IDP and then fuck it all up by simply defaulting back to the search for what sounds good.

By the time you've reached this stage of the IDP, you know a hell of a lot about your customers' needs and wants. You also know those needs and wants are filtered through a plethora of competing pressures, which you have now validated. The problem is that with all that knowledge, it is easy to get overconfident and to rush, simply listing the pressures and putting an intervention against each of them.

Down that path lies madness. It is entirely possible for a single pressure to give rise to many interventions and equally possible for one intervention to satisfy many pressures. Indeed, that's very much the point of the mapping: by formalizing our understanding of pressures, we can more easily see how to combine and sort them. Intervention design is really just the translation of pressures into something we can actually create; if pressures are the levers, interventions are how we pull them, hopefully in the right order and with the right strength.

Let's take an example from my work at Clover Health. As a Medicare Advantage insurance company, our business model is predicated on improving the health outcomes of our members. Surprisingly often, that means getting them to do very basic things that protect their health, like getting a flu shot. About 70 percent of flu hospitalizations and 85 percent of flu deaths occur in those over age sixty-five, which is the majority of the Medicare-eligible population. So particularly for them, fewer flu shots equals more hospitalizations equals more deaths.

Creating behavior change around flu shots is even more important for Clover because, on average, blacks are significantly less likely to get a flu shot than their white counterparts (because medical racism is real). And compared with most Medicare Advantage plans, Clover serves an unusual demographic mix of members: we have about twice as many people of color as the average plan (Medicare in general is insanely white, at about 80 percent), and a substantial portion of that cohort are black.

Enter the IDP. We wrote a behavioral statement with blacks as our population and flu shot as the behavior, then did the insights work and mapped the pressures for some very consistent themes. There was a strong lack of promoting pressures ("Why do I need one? I'm healthy") but, more importantly, several inhibiting pressures that, while present in nonblack populations, were more significant for black people.

For example, people are often somewhat distrustful of the flu shot because it changes every year. There are good reasons for the changing formula (it is based on predictions about what flu strains will be most prevalent in a given year, maximizing the overall efficacy of the shot), but it makes it feel unpredictable, like there is some sort of hidden experimentation going on. And in a world where the Tuskegee Syphilis Study (in which government researchers denied antibiotic treatment to blacks, eventually killing many of them, so that they could continue to study the disease—medical racism to the extreme and beyond fucked up) ended only forty years ago, hidden experimentation is understandably a much more powerful inhibiting pressure among the black population.

This is magnified by the fact that the flu shot can sometimes have side effects, like mild arm pain at the injection site. This is rare—it happens in only about 1 percent of cases—but because you have to get the shot every year, and everyone needs to get it, it is highly likely that you or someone you know has felt those effects in recent memory. A doctor (who is probably white) walking up to a perfectly healthy person and giving them a shot that makes them sick is not exactly winning over hearts and minds in the black community.

And then there is the fact that the flu shot isn't 100 percent effective. Now, that's not quite fair: the flu shot is always effective, in that it will always help you avoid or reduce the effects of the flu. Even if you get the flu, it goes from a weeklong ordeal without a shot to a twenty-four-hour bug with one. But it doesn't guarantee that you won't get the flu, and that's generally what we expect from vaccines: if you get a tetanus shot, you don't get tetanus, full stop.

So we've got the flu shot, which saves lives, burdened by a significant cloud of suspicion because it is entirely unlike most other forms of medicine. You take it when you are healthy, you have to do it repeatedly, and you never quite know if it works because you don't know if you would have gotten sick if you hadn't gotten it. In a country where medical racism is a reality for many blacks, that means lower vaccination rates and more deaths.

Now, in a *Mad Men* world we'd instantly start brainstorming for interventions that sound good. Maybe we could get Beyoncé to tweet about the importance of flu shots! Or have the whistle-blower from Tuskegee write an op-ed! Or anything else that ends in an exclamation point!

But I didn't even fully list the pressures. What about cost? Pure availability? The fact that it has to be done at a specific time and place by a medical professional? The fact that it hurts and many of us are scared of needles? Boring changes behavior as often as sexy does, so avoid spending too long focusing on any one pressure. Keep a careful eye on momentum and recognize when it is causing confirmation bias; we get excited (hence all the exclamation points) and then just start selectively attending to the things that keep us on a roll.

The key at this point in intervention design is volume. If you're facilitating, this is where you want to introduce breaks, flip the direction of the behavioral statement, focus on individual pressures or on combining novel ones, create artificial limitations and what-ifs—anything and everything you can do to get as many interventions on the board as possible, so long as they are directly mapped to the pressures that underlie them.

You will also likely have to remind the group that the goal is not practicality. We're living in a counterfactual world and nothing should be taken as unachievable at this point; we'll have plenty of time to be choosy during intervention selection, and we can always scale back a strong intervention to fit resource constraints. There may also be a tendency to say things like "I don't think that will work," so you'll need to remind you team that is what pilot/test/scale is for. The proof of whether an intervention can change behavior is whether it does and you won't know that until you do it.

With the flu shot we started by grouping—trying to find a single intervention that honored many pressures. Doubts about efficacy, experimentation, and side effects all are broadly affected by trust; was there a single intervention we could use that would create trust? Cost and availability are related, because getting somewhere specific at a specific time usually involves at least some money for transportation or wage loss; was there some synergy there?

When we ran out of intervention ideas, we started siloing—looking for the pressure that showed up in both quantitative and qualitative research and seemed to dominate all others, that we could create several interventions around. For blacks and the flu shot, lack of trust in the medical establishment was the standout inhibiting pressure. Flu shots are free with Clover and available at any pharmacy, but even when members had easy access at clinics that were literally on their own street, the trust issues dominated.

Fortunately, we had already done some work on what is trusted in the older black community. We had read the research, run surveys, talked to our members, and looked at data on nodes of influence. And for those who were least likely to get a flu shot, there was a consistent response: church. "I believe what my congregation believes."

Great, so that was clear: we needed religious leaders on board. We could draft letters for them to send, have them mention the importance of flu shots and caring for the temple of the body during service, have a flu shot drive as a church fundraiser, or any of almost endless ways to draft off their status in the community. Again, the focus was just getting a diversity of interventions on the board, because that's what powers great behavior change.

And there were plenty of other, non-faith-based interventions proposed as well. For example, at Clover we had a fairly unique data set in our Personal Health Motivation question:

an open-ended statement from most of our members about why being healthy was important to them. So in a world where members lacked a clear motivation to get a flu shot, we could readily provide a personalized one in their own words, be it love for grandkids or spouse, desire to be physically active, even (as one member said) to stay out of the hospital in order to feed the stray cats in the neighborhood. When all was said and done, the intervention design process yielded twenty or so unique interventions, which is fairly typical for most IDPs.

Which brings us to the worst and most subjective part of the entire IDP: intervention selection. Because ultimately, even with all the insights and pressures and research, you have to make a judgment call about which interventions you're actually going to bring to pilot (because logistically you can't pilot everything). And unlike almost every other part of the process, there is no exact science here—ultimately, this is where you have to simply place bets.

But you can make them smart bets. Because although you can't pilot everything, you also shouldn't pilot only one thing. Intervention selection isn't about driving to a single solution but rather about setting yourself up for a range of pilots that maximize the chances of creating behavior change. Because good behavioral science, like all good science, is based on the assumption that your interventions won't work.

That last sentence is the one that most often makes people want to fire me (my charming disposition aside). It is a very,

very hard thing to be about a month into a project and have your CBO say that they've selected several pilots that they expect to fail. But that culture of skepticism is important. Remember what we're fighting against: confirmation bias and our natural tendency to believe something is true simply because we want to justify the effort. Hello, *Mad Men*, it is the Vietnam War calling. It wants its sunk cost back.

In selecting multiple interventions, you're shooting for something psychologists call optimum distinctiveness: a range of options that together cover as much of the spectrum as possible, but with relatively little overlap. Imagine you're trying to find a jam you like. Suboptimal distinctiveness is strawberry, raspberry, and strawberry-raspberry. Tasting those three gives you almost no information about the vast plethora of other jams in the world, and good luck trying to figure out which one of the three is best, since they are essentially the same. To find what is right for you, you want an arrangement like strawberry, marmalade, and kiwi—clearly differentiated such that by trying all three, you learn a lot about what works for you and what doesn't.

To reduce your option set, you can do a few things to make it easier. First, combine interventions. For flu shots, we knew trust was important to address and faith-based efforts had a lot of support. We also knew that physical availability and convenience were important to reducing inhibiting pressures around physiological and actual costs. So we took the intervention of faith-based support and the intervention of a flu clinic and put them together—we could put a flu shot clinic in the church itself, since everyone is already there. We also needed a stronger promoting pressure that sidestepped the idea that getting a flu shot is only for the sick—what if we reminded people that you can only get the flu from people who have the flu and that by getting a shot, you can protect the rest of the congregation, many of whom might not be as healthy as you are?

The trick was that even while we referred to "a flu shot clinic in a historically black church on a Sunday with a reminder about protecting the congregation" as one intervention, it combined the strength of many pressures and smaller interventions as well. If we'd had a longer time line, we could have piloted each of the individual parts (clinic versus faith-based endorsement versus messaging about protecting friends and family), but we didn't necessarily have to, because all that matters is whether the overall intervention works. Remember, the goal is behavior change, not knowledge—we don't have to know precisely which part of an intervention drives the behavior, so long as the overall intervention is scalable and results in worthwhile behavior change. It is easy to get obsessed with the magic ingredient and it can save you some resources if you find it, but it isn't required.

We can also start to scale down interventions during this combining process. While driving to every member's house to give them a flu shot was a valid potential intervention, it simply wasn't going to happen. Flu vaccines have to be refrigerated and administered by someone with appropriate clinical licensure, and not every member even wanted us in their home. We still wanted this intervention on the board, but only to take what was good about it (convenience and personalization and the feeling of care) and feed it in to some of our larger combined interventions.

You can also start to look at coverage. Is there an intervention that will work for only a portion of the population? That can be created only under very specific circumstances? That is available only at certain times? In general, if you've done your job while writing your behavioral statement and defined the right population, then intervention selection is about identifying the cheapest, easiest-to-create, most broadly reaching interventions that still change the behavior.

This all may sound highly unnatural, but I promise that, even if it is the most ambiguous step, intervention selection is surprisingly intuitive. Most of your nonconscious brain is busily chunking away on precisely these kinds of trade-offs all the time: we pair complementary flavors in cooking, triangulate location/cost/proximity to our favorite takeout places in finding a place to live, and make a million other daily decisions that we don't even realize we are making. We are machines built for grouping and trading off, but it works only if we create the space for that process to play out.

———

The key is to stay focused on the behavior you are trying to change. So in intervention selection, assume nothing. What worked elsewhere may not work here; what has failed in another context may be viable in this one. Stay fixated on optimal distinctiveness so that you can maximize the chances that you'll find at least some behavior change and move forward from there.

Which brings me to my dinner with Andre(s). Andres Glusman was the VP of product at Meetup, a website that helps local organizers run hundreds of thousands of interest-based events. I met him because we were both giving talks at the same data conference and he shared an example that has become one of my favorites of intervention selection done well; you can probably still watch it on YouTube but I'll summarize here.

This particular example came at a time when Meetup was growing so rapidly that spam was increasingly a major problem. Marketers would create meet ups that were actually just sales pitches for their products, diluting Meetup's interest-organizing behavioral goal. The team was designing interventions to combat spam when the CEO, Scott Heiferman, suggested adding a required checkbox to the meet up creation flow that read "I pledge to create real, face-to-face community."

Andres was skeptical. Sure, it might keep out the spammers, but the golden rule of designing sign-up flows is that you don't add anything unnecessary, because every additional step introduces greater inhibiting pressure and thus lowers the behavior that is registration. But he recognized that the checkbox also reiterated the company's mission and that meet-up organizers are a passionate group; maybe they wouldn't be deterred and the extra inhibiting pressure would be enough to reduce spam. And he did what is critical in intervention selection: he remained open to being proven wrong.

Hopefully, because it is in this book, you've already guessed the counterintuitive (and potentially counterrational) outcome: not only did the checkbox reduce spammers, but it actually increased the number of successfully created meet-ups by 16 percent. Because not only are meet-up organizers sufficiently passionate (promoting pressure) to overcome a checkbox (inhibiting pressure), but reminding them of that passion created additional meaning and actually strengthened the promoting pressure. And the only reason Meetup ever found that out is that Andres had the courage to put aside assumptions carried over from other populations and contexts and just pilot an intervention based directly on clear pressures. Not because it was cool to do or would be cool if it worked but because he knew what behavior he was trying to create and he understood the pressures that created it well enough to take a smart risk.

6.

ETHICAL CHECK

Everything we create, we create to change behavior. And some of our most lauded roles in life are explicitly about behavior change: teacher, doctor, parent, etc. Yet we never talk about them as behavior-changing, and to accuse someone of trying to consciously change the behavior of others is to slander them; the creepy factor is high. It conjures up images of marketers and manipulators and salesmen, rubbing their hands together and laughing maniacally while they addict us to cigarettes or credit cards or sugary drinks.

The reason for the stigma surrounding explicit behavior change goes back to another one of those miracles of human psychology. Our brain has evolved to protect our fragile egos with a number of biases that are remarkably effective despite violating basic logic. One of them is a self-serving bias that goes roughly like this: when I do good things, it is because I'm a good person, but when I do bad things, it is because I was affected by my environment. The reverse is true of others: when they do good, it is because of their environment, while their bad deeds are because they suck and are terrible people.

This helps support our notion of a just world. When other people get raped, it is because they dressed provocatively (which, when you step back from it, is the dumbest fucking thing I've ever heard). When other people are fat, it is because they are lazy. When other people are paid less than a living wage, it is because they are stupid. And because we are not stupid, or lazy, or provocatively dressed, we are safe.

Except sometimes we also do bad things, so we need to conjure a boogeyman to overcome our basic goodness, the devil that made us do it. Enter the behavior-changing villain. Those manipulating marketers created a world that changed our behavior, because we are so good and pure and lovely that we would never have gorged on too much sugar if they hadn't tricked us into it. Thus the paradox of needing to believe in both free will and behavior change (so we can preserve our ego and denigrate others; yep, humans are natural assholes).

ETHICAL CHECK

The reality is less paradoxical: If we set aside our bias, both those angelic teachers and those demonic marketers are behavioral scientists and changing behavior is not, in and of itself, inherently ethical or unethical. Interventions can be used for great good by helping us act on our motivations, and the widespread application of ethical interventions is one of the most promising roads to a better world (no zealot like a convert, remember?). But because interventions can be used to harm others, whether or not you plan to present yourself to the world as someone specializing in behavior change, it is incumbent on each of us to use processes like the IDP responsibly. Remember, behavior change is a war between opposing sides who are invested in specific outcome behaviors, and you should choose consciously which side you're on. Your interventions will always appear ethical when filtered through the lens of your own values, but by understanding some of the potential issues, you can avoid waking up and finding that you aren't proud of the work you've done. Because while the IDP is designed to help you stay on the straight and narrow, it can only go so far—ultimately, we each have to take responsibility for the behavioral outcomes we create.

That's why, having selected what interventions we intend to pilot, we need to stop and do an ethical check based on two factors: *what* behavior we are changing and *how* we are changing behavior. And these ethical problems are mapped to the two fundamental behavioral gaps: the intention-action gap and the intention-goal gap.

Most of us are familiar with the intention-action gap, as it is the dominant problem that behavioral science books concern themselves with: We intend to go to the gym but we don't go to the gym. Want to eat right but end up sitting in front of a bowl of Flamin' Hot Cheetos mixed with M&M's. Meant to write this book like two years ago but, you know, *life* . . . We shrug and battle on.

If we're following the IDP, the *what* ethical problem is solved for the intention-action gap because of the inclusion of a motivation in the behavioral statement. By explicitly aligning the outcome behavior with an originating motivation, we ensure there is no ethical concern that we are forcing a behavior on an unwilling population, because they have already endorsed it. They want to go to the gym, so the only possible ethical issue is in *how* we get them to do that.

The intention-goal gap is less often mentioned in behavioral science but is actually the more ethically fraught. In it we have an explicit outcome we want but have no intention of doing the behavior that leads to it. Want six-pack abs but have no intention of doing crunches. Want to stay healthy but won't wash our hands. Want a bae but refuse to shower. (Ah, teenagers. Also, when I asked people online for the most inclusive version of "significant other," "bae" was the pick—"lover" was the other top suggestion, but "want a lover" just sounds weird.)

The motivation component of a behavioral statement can't help us in this case, because the person has already rejected the behavior as a method for honoring that motivation. Thus we have to deal both with *what* and then with *how*, since solving an intention-goal gap still leaves the potential for an intention-action gap. So let's start with *what* and the intention-goal conundrum.

Determining the ethics in an intention-goal gap situation has a very simple rule: *if your outcome behavior is not the result of any of the motivations of the population, it is unethical.* To put it differently, if you can't construct a valid behavioral statement, you're out of bounds.

To make this easier to see in practice, rewind to our flu shot example. The standard script for changing behavior around the flu shot is ridiculous: a medical professional, whom you supposedly trust, says, "Have you had your flu shot yet? No?"—slaps you on the hand—"You should really get a flu shot" (and people wonder why less than half of Americans get a flu shot). The problem with this approach is that it doesn't actually differentiate between intention-action and intention-goal gaps. So at Clover we tried something obvious but apparently revolutionary: we started asking about intent. In a survey, we asked our members if they got a flu shot last year and, if not, whether they had intended to. And it turned out about 50 percent of members had had every intention of getting a flu shot and didn't (because it wasn't available at their pharmacy, they never got time, etc.), and 50 percent never had any intention of getting a flu shot in the first place. Put differently, half of them had an intention-action gap and half of them had an intention-goal gap.

So the *what* problem here is "Is it ethical to change the behavior of people who said they had no intention of getting the flu shot?" To try to answer that, let's structure the actual intention-goal gap (they want to stay healthy but they don't want to get a flu shot) and talk through solutions.

The first step to determining whether it is ethical is to ensure that the intention-goal gap is clear to the population, because someone may have a goal but not intend to do the associated behavior simply because they don't realize the two are related. For example, if I want to be healthy but don't know the flu shot will help me stay that way, then the gap is simply a problem of information, and making the connection clear will be sufficient to eliminate the gap. Fortunately, you can easily test this: in our flu shot example, we asked if people knew that the flu shot kept them healthy and, because most of them did, we could be sure that the intention-goal gap was not based simply on a lack of education. Indeed, information is very rarely the cause of the intention-goal gap, which is why education-based interventions don't tend to work as often as we'd hope.

Where does that leave us? We know people want to be healthy but don't want to get the flu shot, and they are aware that the two are related. So we cannot ethically change the behavior because the behavioral statement "When [population] wants to stay healthy, and they [limitations], they will get a flu shot (as measured by [data])" isn't true. What we can ethically do is find another motivation.

Remember, the rule is that the behavior change is unethical if it does not honor *any* of the population's motivations, not simply if it doesn't honor the most obvious one. In the case of the flu shot, we had members' stated personal health goals, so rather than a motivation like "stay healthy," we could use a motivation like "keep others healthy." This was ethically fine, because the member had freely expressed a motivation that could be honored with the behavior and the most common health goals are actually about other people— grandkids, kids, spouses, church congregations, and all the other people that make us want to be healthy, simply so we can hang out with them.

Now, that seems obvious enough, but it is also easy to talk ourselves around. For example, a cigarette marketer might simply say that everyone wants to look cool and that smoking makes you look cool, and thus it is ethically fine to create the behavior that is smoking. Which is why we need a second clause to make the rule more complete: *if your outcome behavior is not the result of any of the population's motivations or the benefit of that behavior does not outweigh the cost to an alternative motivation, it is unethical.*

The flu shot meets this requirement: it honors a motivation ("keep others healthy") without significantly impeding any other motivations. Smoking does not pass the test, because while it may make you look cool, and most people want that, it also kills you, and most people are decidedly anti-dying. The minimal amount of extra cool you get is decidedly outweighed by the extra death.

But we've only resolved half of the ethical dilemma; we now know *what* behaviors we can change, but we haven't delineated *how* it is ethical to change them. Fortunately, that is only another twist of the statement away. In addition to the benefit of one behavior not outweighing the cost to another, the same can be said of interventions. So our statement becomes *If your outcome behavior is not the result of any of the motivations of the population or the benefit of that behavior or intervention does not outweigh the cost to an alternative motivation, it is unethical.*

For example, imagine that our flu-shot letters contained extreme language about protecting others, like "Your not getting a flu shot will kill your grandchildren." First, that's a lie. But second, it will likely make people feel extremely sad and angry, when people are motivated to feel the opposite, so the cost to happiness exceeds the benefit of a flu shot. And thus it is unethical.

Now, you might correctly point out that our cigarette marketer is left with rather a lot of room to equivocate here and you'd be right; as with all the many biases we've discussed in this book, even the most well-intentioned person can talk themselves into things, because the brain is built to manipulate our perception to support our actions. And we'll never be completely able to eliminate that, despite our inclusion of the motivation in the behavioral statement and all the other guardrails we've set in place. So let's add one more clause to our statement to help set up an additional defense: transparency.

Since our statement has a subjective component (the cost/benefit ratio), it is inherently true that different people may evaluate that trade-off differently. The cigarette marketer, whose livelihood depends on the interventions they create, is under significant cognitive pressure to undervalue costs and overstate benefits. By being transparent about both our behavioral statement and our interventions, we allow for the ethics to be evaluated by people who do not have the same motivations that we do. Just as we triangulate with different research methods to achieve convergent validity on a reality, we can triangulate with different cost/benefit evaluations to achieve convergent validity on ethics. And as noted before,

START AT THE END

the wider the variety of the evaluations, the more confident we can be in the outcome.

Now, there may be reasons that full transparency is impossible: business considerations or laws or even the fact that some interventions are diminished in effectiveness if they are made overly transparent. It is incumbent on all behavioral scientists to push that boundary as much as possible, getting as close to fully transparent as we can. That can mean getting opinions widely within your own organization, consulting with experts in the field, or engaging an external ethical entity, like an institutional review board. At Clover, for example, members of the behavioral science team complete ethics training, we have an internal ethical review committee chaired by our Chief Science Officer and with representation from across the organization and, most important, we make every effort to publish our interventions, regardless of whether they work or not, on our public blog.

Now we've got a sentence that is easier to read if we bullet it out.

If:

- your outcome behavior is not the result of any of the population's motivations
- or the benefit of your outcome behavior or an intervention to produce it does not outweigh the cost to an alternative motivation

92

- or you are unwilling to publicly describe and take responsibility for the outcome behavior or intervention
- it is unethical.

And with transparency and responsibility in our statement, it is finally a reasonable ethical check. It isn't foolproof and we must always be conscious of confirmation bias and the tendency to believe that our interventions are ethical simply because they are ours. As mentioned repeatedly throughout this book, staying focused on your outcomes and being wary of your love of any specific intervention is one of the most important skills of a behavioral scientist.

Having reduced the inhibiting pressure to doing it right, let's increase the promoting pressure by scaring the hell out of you, shall we? April 2, 2017. Noam Scheiber writes a story for *The New York Times* revealing Uber's use of behavioral science to keep drivers on the road long past when it was safe for them to continue driving.[9] Uber, in a lovely reflection of the culture Travis set up, actually defends itself with the following:

> "We show drivers areas of high demand or incentivize them to drive more," said Michael Amodeo, an Uber spokesman. "But any driver can stop work literally at the tap of a button—the decision whether or not to drive is 100 percent theirs."

Who the fuck says something like that? To be clear, "But they have free will!" is a bad defense of any intervention. By creating specifically to produce a behavior change, you accept responsibility for the result of that behavior change. Just as tobacco companies can't simply say "But people can stop smoking at any time" as they spend billions on advertising that they know makes stopping harder, Uber can't simply say "But people can stop driving at any time" when they deliberately designed a product to make stopping harder. The benefit of staying on the road does not outweigh the cost of dying in a car accident or becoming a nervous wreck.

My favorite part of Uber's defense, however, was claiming that the interventions shouldn't be concerning because they don't work. Jonathan Hall, Uber's head of economic and policy research, argued in *The New York Times* story that "exploiting people's psychological tics was unlikely to have more than a marginal effect on how long they played Zynga's games or drove for Uber." Really? Then stop doing it. If the benefit does not explicitly outweigh the cost to the population on which you are intervening, always err on the side of not scaling the intervention.

Since we're picking on tech companies, let's go with another fan favorite: Facebook. In June 2014 they, along with some Cornell researchers, published a paper[10] that revealed a massive intervention in which the company manipulated the contents of users' newsfeeds to contain either more positive or more negative content, which then caused users to post more positive or negative content of their own. Yep—Facebook knowingly made people less happy. Fan-fucking-tastic.

As with Uber, Facebook's ludicrous process can help us understand how they ended up running such a transparently unethical intervention. First, they didn't follow the IDP. The intervention was run on nearly 700,000 users, without a strong pilot, when one of the whole reasons we have a pilot is to avoid abrasion from negative activities. If Facebook had piloted this intervention on 100 people and quickly discovered that it made people post more negatively, they could have killed it without damaging the emotional state of 700,000 other people. Particularly galling? The researchers seem proud, noting gleefully in the first sentence of the paper that the sample size was "massive."

Second, they avoided review. The editor of the academic journal in which the study was published released a response to the massive outcry the paper spawned:

> When the authors prepared their paper for publication in PNAS, they stated that: "Because this experiment was conducted by Facebook, Inc. for internal purposes, the Cornell University IRB [Institutional Review Board] determined that the project did not

fall under Cornell's Human Research Protection Program." This statement has since been confirmed by Cornell University.[11]

To translate the academic-speak, Facebook deliberately avoided external review rather than seeking it out. Remember our transparency and responsibility clause; if you find yourself hoping other people don't review your work, you're probably doing something unethical.

Third, they obfuscated in their responses. The researchers themselves apologized almost immediately, not for the negative affect they created through the intervention but for the anxiety publishing the study caused people after the fact. Yep—making people unhappy was totally fine in the intervention itself, but we are really sorry for upsetting you by telling you about it.

Facebook's response would come months later in the form of a blog post from the CTO,[12] who deliberately didn't mention that the company promoted negative content in the intervention, only that it promoted positive content. Again, if you find yourself having to very carefully write a blog post to avoid controversy, you're probably doing something unethical.

In the blog post, the CTO listed actions that Facebook had taken in response to the outcry over the study, including four simple points: the creation of ethical guidelines, an internal ethics review committee with representatives from across the org, ethics training, and a research website on which the company would post its papers in one place (this last one is a bit iffy; agreeing to post your published research papers isn't the same as posting your interventions). Unsurprisingly, those map to tactics I suggested to you earlier—what is completely unclear is why Facebook, which had a $200 billion market cap at the time, hadn't managed to do any of this previously.

In case I haven't made the promoting pressure strong enough: Facebook lost $14 billion and $12 billion in market value in the week after the release of the paper and the blog post, respectively. Correlational but hopefully enough to remind you that your organization and your ethics are inexorably tied together.

7.

PILOT AND PILOT VALIDATION, TEST AND TEST VALIDATION, SCALE DECISION AND CONTINUOUS MEASUREMENT

Every day, at conferences around the world, someone starts a talk by explaining the dictionary definition of a word and how it is problematic. I hate those fucking talks. But they do tap into one of the essential truths of any field: if people don't agree on terms, everything stalls out. So, without using a dictionary, I want to be clear and specific about how I'm using "pilot," "test," and "scale" and why they power three unique stages of the IDP.

First, they go in that order; you can't test something and then pilot it. With each advancement, you gain certainty about the ability of the intervention to actually create behavior change and information about the size and cost of that change. This is in large part because each stage implies a bigger sample size (fancy statistics-speak for "how many people interacted with the intervention"), a more durable design and process, a greater number of your organization's people involved, and a greater likelihood that the intervention is going to become a permanent part of their standard operating procedure.

Pilots are tightly scoped interventions that we expect not to work (remember, we have to explicitly prove efficacy as a defense against confirmation bias), so we use small populations, focus on speed to market, and do them in an operationally dirty way. Besides being fun to say, "operationally dirty" just means that we're shooting for minimal impact on the organization as a whole, not routinizing for scale, because it is highly unlikely that a pilot will go forward without significant iteration and refinement, and thus any resources spent on durable processes are likely to be lost.

This has a surprisingly important secondary benefit: reducing abrasion on both customers and employees. When we do things in what seems like a polished way, customers quickly acclimate and discontinuation feels like a loss. And for employees it is a much harder blow. One of the mistakes leaders often make is forgetting that people invest themselves in what they create and thus expecting that they will be unconcerned when projects are cut. But people care deeply about the meaning of their work, so by keeping pilots small and operationally dirty (yep, still fun to say), you reduce employee abrasion by minimizing investment. In a lovely demonstration of this effect, Dan Ariely and colleagues showed that if you pay people to assemble Legos, they will stop working much sooner if you immediately and visibly disassemble the Lego creations than if you let the subjects line up the completed models in front of them.[13] People want to feel accomplished and so pilots and tests help us control what the definition of an accomplishment is.

Speed and resource efficiency are also important here. Because we chose multiple interventions during intervention selection, we'll likely be running three to five concurrent pilots at any given time. If those pilots are too operationally heavy, we'll stall out, so we have to be constantly focused on finding the lowest-fidelity version of an intervention that will still result in behavior change. My rule of thumb for project managers is that if it takes longer than two weeks to get into the field, you need to scale it back and go smaller. Think you'll eventually want to do this at scale with a letter, but the mail room is backed up? Start with a phone call. Imagine a fancy, tech-enabled process? Show positive traction with a spreadsheet and some elbow grease first. But again, make sure it is enough to actually produce the behavior change; you don't want to falsely reject an intervention simply because you rushed it.

Pilot validation is just like insight validation: qualitative and quantitative confirmation that you're headed in the right direction. Because of the small N, it won't be statistically significant, but that's fine; you're just trying to get enough of a positive/negative/null signal to make a decision about what comes next. Did some people get flu shots at our church clinic who wouldn't have otherwise? Did more people who got our letters get flu shots than didn't? Get a rough idea, triangulate it, and move on. Or if it is truly null and you have the instinct that it simply is about not having enough signal, you can always enlarge a pilot and run it again.

Even if we're not shooting for significance, pilot validation is one of the most important phases of the IDP for measurement. When we wrote our behavioral statement, we said confident things like "as measured by [data]," but the pilot is the first time we'll actually measure the behavior. Quantitative researchers will figure out how to actually get that data in a durable way and qualitative researchers start to understand what questions to ask in their interview script and what environments are the right ones for observation. Done right, the instrumentation we build now will carry us through until we make a scaling decision.

It is highly likely that some of your interventions will give you a null result or possibly even cause the opposite of the behavior change that you were working toward. And that's to be expected; if everything we try creates the behavior change we want, it is likely that we are measuring wrong or falling victim to confirmation bias. When an intervention doesn't create the behavior change you want, you've got a decision to make. And like intervention selection, this one is something you ultimately just have to intuit: either you revise the pilot and rerun or you kill it and return to your pressure map and intervention design. But, again as with intervention selection, some patterns can help inform the decision.

Hopefully you've followed the IDP and run multiple pilots, often with common pressures behind them. So you can look at whether a pilot's failure was singular or part of a larger pattern. For example, say I have religious leaders give sermons on the importance of protecting others by getting a flu shot and I write personalized letters to people based on the same promoting pressure of community responsibility, and neither intervention shows even the slightest sign that it's working. That might be evidence that community responsibility isn't as strong a pressure as I thought and I should discontinue pilots in that direction. On the other hand, if the sermons work and the letters don't, that tells me that community responsibility still might be powerful and I should revise the letter pilot to be more like the sermon.

The decision to revise can also be affected by how successful other interventions are in the mix, even if they're not based on the same pressure. Ultimately, we don't care about the fate of any individual intervention or even the validation of a pressure; they are all means to an end. We start at the end and the end is behavior. So if you run five interventions and one of them doesn't work but the other four have great effect sizes, don't spare the lost intervention a second thought and move on. You've changed behavior, and that is what the whole IDP is for.

Now, I slipped in "statistically significant" and "effect size" earlier, and some of you nodded along even though you actually have no idea what the fuck those terms mean. Don't worry, I do that whenever someone starts talking about pop culture; I can't pick your average teen pop star out of a lineup. But the stats actually matter here and understanding them will make you a better steward of the IDP, so we're going to take a brief foray into statistics and how we use them before continuing on with pilot/test/scale. I'm not actually going to teach you how to do any math (what kind of book do you think this is?), but I'm at least going to make sure that you can nod along for real.

Even if you're a stats expert, read this part, since I'm going to challenge some basic assumptions here. I'm a modern

Mulder; they've been lying to you about p-values your whole life! It's a conspiracy!

The statistics we use for validating interventions are based on the simple fact that people are neither perfectly predictable nor perfectly unpredictable. If we were perfectly predictable, we wouldn't need any statistics, because there would be zero variability in the effect of an intervention on a population. Think of our personalized flu shot letter; if humans were perfectly predictable, then either everyone who got a letter would get a flu shot or none of them would. So validation would be as easy as simply observing which way the entire group moves.

If people were perfectly unpredictable, we also wouldn't need math (or interventions), because the IDP would no longer work. No matter what flu shot intervention we ran, people would just randomly get shots or not without any regard for pressures. In that the world has not yet descended into chaos and behavior change actually works, we can safely assume it is not an entirely unpredictable world.

And so we send the letter, and some people get flu shots and some people don't. What statistics helps us do is figure out how much of that difference in behavior is due to the letter and how much is due to all the other pressures that might cause people to get or not get a flu shot.

In a perfect world, we'd send the letter to everyone on earth. That way, when we measured the behavior change, we'd know exactly how strong the intervention was because we'd know its true effect on the entire population. But that's obviously not going to happen; I can't pay for 7.5 billion letters! So instead we send it to some people (our sample, of "sample size" fame) and try to generalize to what everyone else will do. The more people we send it to, the more confident we can be that the results we measure would hold true if we sent it to everyone.

For a pilot, we could take two hundred people and send one hundred of them a letter (the treatment group) and do nothing for the other one hundred (the control group). Then we can do two types of statistical tests to tell if the letter was effective at changing their behavior. The first is a within-subjects test: we take just the people who got the letter, and we see how many of them got a shot in the month before the letter and how many got a shot in the month after. If more got the shot after getting the letter than before, we have some evidence it might have worked.

But wait! It might just be true that the later in the flu season it is, the more people go get flu shots, and it had nothing to do with the letter. So we can do a between-subjects test to triangulate: we see how many of the people who got the letter got a flu shot in the month after and how many people who didn't get a letter got a flu shot in the month after. If more got the shot in the letter group than in the no-letter group, again we have some evidence it might have worked.

Hopefully both of those comparisons point in the same direction: that getting a letter makes it more likely that people get a flu shot. Not perfectly likely (remember our only-sort-of-predictable people) but more likely than if we'd done nothing at all. Which leads to two important questions: "How much more likely does the flu shot letter make people to get a shot?" and "How can we be sure that this will generalize beyond these two hundred people?" This is why there are two numbers your quantitative research is likely to report: an effect size and a p-value.

Effect size answers the first question: it tells you whether the letter was really good at getting people to change their behavior or if it only changed their behavior a little bit. Interpreting an effect size is pretty straightforward in that the higher the number, the more effective the intervention, and while it isn't immediately obvious what the actual effect size means (it depends heavily on what you're measuring), a quantitative researcher can easily translate it into a descriptive statement like "20 percent more people will get a flu shot after getting a letter."

The p-value answers the second question: it tells you how confident you can be that the letter actually caused the effect. It is a little confusing because a lower number means you can be more certain an intervention worked, in that p-value is actually the percentage chance that whatever you thought you saw in the population was really just due to random variation and not your intervention. So if I say the letter causes people to get a flu shot and the p-value is 0.2, that means there is a 20 percent chance I'm wrong (and the letter has no effect) and an 80 percent chance I'm right (and the letter changes behavior). Note that being wrong doesn't mean the letter has a negative effect and actually stops people from getting a shot, just that it doesn't do anything at all, which we call a null result.

Now this is where you might have to get in a fight if you're forced to use a data science team that you haven't groomed for work on behavior change. The conventional p-value that we take as "real" is p < 0.05 (a 5 percent chance you're wrong, or one in twenty). But that convention comes from academia, where it is incredibly important that we don't ever report anything that isn't true, because other people will build their research on top of it and a wrong result could invalidate the whole damn house of cards.

We care about changing behavior, not the gnostic pursuit of knowledge. So we can afford to be rightish. Imagine the following: I have an intervention where p = 0.2. If you say that to the average data scientist, they will tell you that you have nothing. *Good God, man! There is a one in five chance you're wrong. Humbug, humbug, humbug.*

But you didn't ask me about the intervention! It is a pill that is small and easy to swallow, with no side effects of any kind other than making you 20 percent more attractive. It tastes of cotton candy and rainbows and costs a penny. And it cures fucking cancer. Think maybe, even if there is a one in five chance I'm wrong and it doesn't cure cancer, that we might want to look a little further? Because that's all pilot validation is: telling us whether or not we should proceed to a larger test.

For the interventions typically on the table, there are generally few consequences to being wrong other than wasted resources. So it isn't such a terrible thing to be right four out of five times, if the intervention has no significant downsides. And this is where statistics comes back in.

The reason we have p-values is that we can't give the intervention to everyone in the world; if we did, whatever we measured would be the actual effectiveness of the intervention, because we would know exactly how many people changed their behavior. Sampling produces the need for a confidence value, because we are generalizing based on a select, representative population. And the smaller the sample, the more generalizing we are doing: if we did the intervention for half of the world and then measured, we'd be a lot more confident that our measurement represented the true power to change behavior than if we measured for only a hundred people.

And the whole point of a pilot is that it is small. So it is highly, highly unlikely that we will get to a strong confidence of the behavior of the entire population from our little pilot. Which is one of the reasons we do a test.

If you've got convergent validity of behavior change, even at $p = 0.2$, you want to start learning more about the intervention. A test is just like a pilot but with a larger population and greater operational diligence. We're looking hard at the question of "Is it worth it?" in this step, measuring how hard it is going to be to scale against the overall impact it will actually have on behavior. Again, this kills more things than you'd think: it turns out to be relatively easy to find interventions that change behavior but relatively hard to find ones that are worth doing. And the way we know is through test validation; again, that constant quantitative and qualitative feedback is key, though our tests also have to stand up to our requirements about operational cost and effect size.

Now, if you're smart (or a smart-ass), you might ask why we don't just skip directly to a test to begin with, since the larger sample size is always going to give us a better read. After all, if the only thing a pilot does is tell us that we have to run it again but bigger, why not just start big and save ourselves the extra step?

Because I said so. And because not going directly to scale is really cheap insurance against all sorts of obvious harms, like wasting money on scaled interventions that don't change behavior and avoiding the perceptual harm of doing something both big and stupid. But you could argue that a test would have caught these issues and been only slightly more expensive/less exposing than a pilot. So why pilot if we care about p-values?

The real reason boils down to a simple human truth: losing hurts. And bigger losses hurt more. The more effort we put into something, the more desperate we get not to lose, so the more we ignore evidence that an intervention might not be working. It all comes back to that confirmation bias that we are trying so hard in the IDP to guard against. The primary advantage of pilots is not that they are small but that they require less effort than tests, which makes us more willing to recognize interventions that don't change behavior.

It isn't just saving money on flu shot letter postage or avoiding brand embarrassment. Remember that pilots are deliberately operationally dirty, to avoid both large investments of resources and disruptions to existing processes. In modern business, a shocking number of interventions are rolled out at scale with neither piloting nor testing, yet almost no one would say that testing is a bad idea. The reason we don't do more of it is the strength of the inhibiting pressure of effort, not the weakness of the promoting pressure of value. So by reducing effort with easier pilots, we create more cycles of intervention validation.

Let's use Clover as an example of how this difference plays out with some simple math. My behavioral science team organizes our members into pods of three: one quantitative researcher, one qualitative researcher, and one project manager. They work on two projects at a time, an average of eight weeks per project, so roughly twelve projects per year. Each project generally pilots between 3 and 5 interventions, so that's 36 to 60 pilots a year. We usually have between 2 and 3 pods running, for a grand total of up to 180 pilots for a ten-person team.

Imagine trying to test that many interventions, in an operationally clean way, at large enough scale that you get to $p < 0.05$. Leaving aside that you likely couldn't sustain that pace simply because there would be no such thing as standard operation procedure (remember, that's three operationalized changes a week), think about yourself as a leader. Would you have the fortitude to admit that 50 percent of those interventions didn't change behavior and should be terminated? Even if you could, your team would all defect, since you spent all their time on projects that didn't scale.

Pilots let us make light bets that don't demand a lot of commitment and nothing kills the confirmation bias faster. By putting a step before tests and running so many pilots outside our normal operations, we avoid advocating for appealing but bad ideas, simply because we weren't that invested in the first place and have plenty of other things to try.

Which is why we don't mind $p = 0.2$ at the pilot stage.

Coupled with strong qualitative triangulation, it is enough to move forward to a test and take the hit of an operational disruption to see how we might do an intervention at scale. And that's really where tests shine. In a pilot, we're not even trying to pretend that we are doing something in a sustainable way; the sole objective is to figure out whether behavior is changed at all. In a test, we can really start to consider what it would be like for something to become part of our standard operating procedure.

That causes a few things to happen at the test stage. First, because we are now operationalizing for real, we will likely refine the intervention. Part of that is due to learnings gathered during the pilot, but part of it is just the necessary changes that happen as we move something toward scalability. And we'll validate so we can ensure that none of the changes modified that ultimate outcome.

Second, more people are going to get exposed to the intervention, certainly customers but also your own employees. This matters mostly because of that pesky confirmation bias problem. We've now seen an intervention work once in pilot, so we're excited and people are going to want to push it forward. But remember, $p = 0.2$ means there is a 20 percent chance that the intervention doesn't actually change behavior, so 20 percent of interventions at that level shouldn't pass test validation (if they do, you've got a confirmation bias problem). When that happens, you've got a similar choice to the failure of a pilot validation: rerun it and see if it is just an outlier, kill it entirely because other interventions are working, or send it back to pilot to try modifications. You'll look at p-value and effect size and possible interferences and make a choice that may not be popular because of the expanded exposure. Welcome to being a leader.

Still, $p = 0.2$ means that 80 percent of the time the intervention did work and you're going to show that again during test validation. But test is about more than just confirming that the intervention changes behavior; it is also about deciding whether it is worth doing. Is the juice worth the squeeze? Because the primary outcome of a test is not an intervention but a scale decision.

At this point in the IDP, we've done multiple rounds of validation, extending from our very earliest insights and pressure mapping all the way to not one but two different validations of the actual intervention in the real world. We also have an idea of how much effort the intervention will take to deploy. So taken together, after the test, we can make a fairly strong juice/squeeze statement that sounds something like this:[14]

We are [confidence] that [intervention] will [direction] [behavior] (as measured by [data]). Scaling this requires [effort] and will result in [change].

Aren't Mad Libs fun? Let's do the decoding.

Confidence = based on p-value but phrased colloquially

Intervention = what the intervention is

Direction = whether it increases or decreases the behavior

Behavior = the measurable activity you established in your behavior statement

Data = how you quantify that your population is doing the behavior

Effort = the resources required to scale

Change = based on p-value but phrased colloquially

For our flu-shot letters, that might look something like:

We are very confident that sending personalized flu shot letters based on member health motivations will increase the rate of getting a flu shot (as measured by flu shot claims). Scaling this requires about ten hours and $5,500 and will result in about five hundred additional flu shots.

Most of the terms are fairly self-explanatory and are the natural result of the steps of the IDP. But there is one subtle addition that the smart smart-asses might point out: why do we need an expression of confidence, if we're supposed to scale only things we're confident in?

The easy answer is that there is confidence and there is *confidence* (which sounds like a tagline for Viagra) and that is true: there is a difference between 85 percent sure and 99 percent sure, and decision makers deserve to know which you are. But there is actually a more important reason: we need to document our failures.

In science, because the method of disseminating results has become primarily peer-reviewed journals, we have a file drawer problem: you never hear about studies with marginal results because they never get published. Indeed, we have plenty of studies that actually do have significant results but still don't make the cut, simply because they're not deemed novel enough and journals are rewarded for being selective.

In business, the file drawer problem is magnified, because not only do we not talk about marginal results or unfunded interventions but we don't talk about results that go the wrong direction. At least in science, if you accidentally discover that some well-accepted phenomenon cannot be replicated or your experiment has the opposite effect, that's publishable. But in business, a lack of strong evidence, an intervention that has the opposite effect, and an inability to get funding are all viewed as failures, and the cardinal rule of business is You Don't Talk About Failures.

Forget that when it comes to the IDP. A scale decision that just as clearly calls out that we're confident that flu letters won't work, or that we're not sure if it will work, is valid and should be archived along with all the other details of the IDP for that intervention. We document the results of every intervention, no matter if it is good, bad, or indifferent.

Imagine if Bing in the Classroom hadn't worked and I'd left Microsoft in disgrace. Like the One Ring (can't resist a hobbit joke), time would have moved on and my efforts would have been forgotten. Which means that eventually, someone else would have had to do the whole damn thing again. Simply by documenting our lack of confidence, or our confidence that we got it wrong, we create a searchable history that becomes an asset for all future interventions. And that, smart-ass, is why we express our confidence.

The rest is easy. We are describing the intervention, the behavior it creates, and the juice/squeeze trade-off. But the fact that the sentence is clear doesn't mean the scale decision will be easy; trading off resources with competing needs is what makes or breaks organizations. But when we drive those needs through the IDP and create interventions where the juice/squeeze is known, prioritizing which interventions to fund becomes more than simply a function of by whom and how a pitch is made.

Tough as the scale decision is, we still aren't done because of a basic truth: even scaled interventions eventually stop working. And the only way to know when they do, and to modify or eliminate them, is to implement continuous monitoring. It is validation all over again, but in an ongoing way that checks on the health not just of one intervention but of our entire behavior-change portfolio.

There are two main reasons why this is important and they both have to do with the fact that for behavioral scientists, there is really only one true limited resource: cognitive attention. And speaking as the father of a three-year-old, my mental resources are shrinking, not growing. Your brain can only process so many things at any given time, and even if we remove them from your active consideration to be handled by the nonconscious mind, you'll eventually run dry. And every intervention, no matter how small, eats up some of that limited pile of cognitive attention.

This causes something we sometimes call the piranha effect. Over time, you'll build up a portfolio of scaled interventions that target the same behavior. For example, think about smoking cessation interventions. Because no one intervention changes everyone's behavior, we have to continually create new ones. And if you added up every academic paper ever written about smoking cessation interventions, the effect size would be massive, which implies that if we just layered those interventions on top of one another, everyone would stop smoking.

Except that isn't what happens. Instead, while each new intervention certainly changes the behavior of some additional people, it doesn't convert the same number that it would have in isolation. This can happen both between interventions that target the same behavior (putting your cigarette pack in a locked drawer steals a little attention from the warning label on it that reminds you that smoking will kill you) and among all the interventions of the world (going on a diet and stopping smoking at the same time? good luck with that). And so by continuously monitoring all our interventions, we can see the effect of each additional one. Does it cannibalize gains from another intervention? Is it more or less effortful? Continuous monitoring lets us titrate our juice to exactly the right blend of squeeze. And that is why having cascading behavioral statements is so useful: if Uber's marketing department does something that gets more app sign-ups but it ultimately drives down overall rides, that's a bad intervention and can safely be pruned out.

Now, some of this is beyond your control. Intervention competition fuels the massive advertising spend I got so mad about in the introduction to this book: badly designed interventions that are not well coordinated cause massive cognitive overload and force a nuclear arms race for attention. And you

START AT THE END

can't really opt out of the global race for cognitive resources, no matter how well you control your internal portfolio.

But again, this is why continuous monitoring helps us. If you are trying to stop smoking behavior and launch an effective portfolio of interventions that does so, that portfolio can be disrupted by shifts in the pressures upon which those interventions are based. The same ads that worked in the 1970s likely won't work the same way fifty years later. Changing pressures may cause you to modify or terminate any number of interventions, and that's just a natural part of the process; despite all the work that went into creating a scaled intervention, it has no inherent right to exist and should be terminated to make room for new and better interventions.

Fortunately, since we documented the entire IDP that produced them, we can work back up the chain to see what has shifted. If all our cost-based interventions suddenly stop working, that's a pretty good sign that the price of alternatives has changed and that is where we need to start from again. The IDP helps our interventions be inherently resilient, but only if we implement the methods to detect change.

Since continuous monitoring is just another form of validation, there isn't an extensive new process to document, so I'll limit myself to one final note: make sure your continuous monitoring has interruptive alerts. A dashboard is not continuous monitoring, because it requires a human to open said dashboard and monitor for change. In the same way that you don't want to waste all the time you spent in the IDP by failing to instrument continuous monitoring, think how it would feel if you had all the right measurement in place but no way to be notified.

And that wraps it up. You'll frequently go through the entire IDP for a particular behavior again at various points as your organization grows, but for the moment, you'll have scaled one or more interventions and achieved enough behavior change that a break is warranted. Remember, we need psychological distance to improve things, so find something else to work on while this one bakes at scale for a bit.

In the *Mad Men* world of today, the decision about what we build is anchored in features that are irrelevant to the quality of interventions and the behavioral outcomes they create. White guys with internal political capital and slick presentation decks pitch leaders who already want to believe them, because the confirmation bias is alive and well in the old boys' club. It sounds good on paper, so it must be good for the company, with no measuring stick for what "good" actually means other than that it came from our fortunate sons. It is a tautology masquerading as a meritocracy, and we all are paying the price.

Inhabit the counterfactual proposed in this book. The deck is simply a walk-through of the IDP, guided by the people who did the research and ran the pilots and tests. It is not a pitch, because we are all on the same side. The fundamentals are not disputed, because we have documented how they were collected and measured them, and the meeting focuses on evaluating tested interventions against one another based on the resources needed and expected outcomes. It is balancing, not selling.

Now choose which world you want to live in. Because there is a whole new way of doing business available and you get to decide for yourself if you're going to be part of it. You can put behavior at the center of your processes and prioritize the interventions that change it. You can start at the end.

8.

THE END OF
THE BEGINNING

really wanted to mic drop at the end of the last chapter. Come on, how great would that be: a lovely, eloquent thirty-thousand-word package on creating behavior change that just happens to cleverly lead to the title of the book itself? Smooth.

And completely unrealistic. I've been doing this at scale longer than almost anyone else, I run one of the most well-staffed internal behavioral science teams in the world, I have strong executive buy-in and excellent operational partners to transition from pilot to test, and even I can't make it look this good. In reality, creating behavior change is messy because our organizations are messy and so are the people we are trying to change. That's not a reason not to do it.

Some of you get it. You'll finish this book and just start doing things differently. You'll be the person on the subway ruminating on how to get everyone to give up their seat to the elderly; you'll start balancing pressures in your mind and connecting them to interventions. Formally or informally, you'll start shifting the culture at your organization toward one of validation, and you'll look for people like you with whom you can divide the work and create the diversity that is so necessary to really doing the IDP well.

To you, I say go forth and multiply. Remember the quote we started the book with: "Far and away the best prize that life has to offer is the chance to work hard at work worth doing." Teddy Roosevelt was talking to a bunch of farmers and mostly being a prick about how noble we working savages are. But Teddy wasn't wrong; abundant science shows us that meaning matters. When his wife died, it was work that saved Teddy's life. Maybe the struggle for behavior change will save yours, as it has surely saved mine.

So give this book to someone else, make your own versions of the IDP, remind the world that if science is their method and behavior their outcome, they too are behavioral scientists. If you need help, shoot me an email (matt@

mattwallaert.com) and we'll see what can be done, because I always have time for those willing to grapple with making things better. Hell, my website even has a link where you can book a call slot with me. No, I don't charge—you asshole— remember, no zealot like a convert. I don't take speaking fees or consulting fees or talking-to-me fees for one very simple reason: I believe that if we do this right, a whole lot of things get a whole lot better. And I hope that you believe that too.

Smart smart-asses that you are, you'll notice there are a lot more pages in this book. That's because I've left you plenty more material to soak in. The rest of the chapters are case studies in behavior change, deep dives on specific pressures, and ruminations on some of the thorny bits you're likely to prick yourself on as you go through this process. They can be read nonlinearly, and don't feel pressured to continue; if you made it here, you've got enough to start the work.

But I know that only some of you are ready for more. Because every time I present the IDP, someone will come up afterward and tell me how they love the idea but why it will never work in their organization. Lack of executive support, lack of resources, not enough of the right kind of people and too many of the wrong kind. I'm sympathetic; those are all strong inhibiting pressures that can make people not want to keep fighting for change.

But that's the whole point of why we are here together. In general, we've spent most of the book so far talking about behavior change as it applies to customers/users/members/ whatever you call people external to your organization. But remember that I talked about the IDP as a universal process for designing for behavior change, precisely because people are people no matter the context. That means, if you got this far and believe in working back from the behavior you want to see, you can shift your organization's behavior exactly as you would your users'. Because your organization is just people, and you know how to change people's behavior.

So if you're feeling stumped, start there. Identify the organizational behavior you believe blocks you from implementing the IDP and write a behavioral statement. Find insights and validate them. Map the pressures and design interventions. And then pilot, pilot, pilot.

And if you do it right, you'll feel it. In a "just ship it" culture, you'll be slower at the beginning, but remember that our only measure of success is the change in behavior. Because you are validating at every step, you're learning. Slow is smooth, smooth is fast, and while they're pivoting around trying to find product market fit, you've got an organized process in which everything you do builds on itself.

Because life invites science. Everything is subject to deliberate change and, having read this book, you now have a process to systematically create that change. You can no longer make the excuse that a behavior cannot be changed because, given enough time and resources, everything can be. Of course, you might still decide some behaviors aren't worth your time, and that's fine; we all have to pick our battles. But be undaunted; you can make this work. Remember that when the right thing is the easy thing, everyone will do the right thing.

We all have power, and while it may vary in degree, there is a zone of control within which each of us has influence. Even if it is starting with changing the behavior of just one person, and even if that person is just you . . . I consider it a challenge before the whole human race, and I ain't gonna lose.

Look at that; I managed to get in a Queen lyric. Now I can drop the mic.

PART 2

ADVANCED
BEHAVIOR
CHANGE

9.

PRIMING, MODERATION, AND MEDIATION

f there is a One Ring of pressures, it is identity (does that mean I'm Sauron?). It is where we spend the majority of our resources, hopefully after basics like food and shelter are taken care of (although judging by the total U.S. consumer debt, probably not). We relentlessly consume identity-related products, from fashion to music to activities, and consumption is only escalating as social media turns literally everything into an act of identity. Forget food as a means of fueling the body—now it has to be a complex expression of who you are!

And it's not just highly industrialized countries; in developing economies, disposable income is growing (thankfully), and as people move away from simple subsistence, there is a corresponding increase in identity spend. Indeed, it is likely that identity-related sales in developing countries will be a significant growth opportunity for both existing brands and new entrants in the coming years.

So it is no accident that the $220 billion advertising spend is mostly focused on identity. Few ads speak solely to the features of a product, but most try to connect the idea of the product to our idea of ourselves. And clearly, it works—organizations aren't stupid, and that spend is well justified as a lever for creating new pressures.

But it does so only through brute force. Ads are interventions delivered in isolation and in the most impoverished medium. To be effective and efficient, identity needs to be situated within all of our interventions, not apart from them, and so almost every highly successful intervention uses identity as a primary pressure.

There are vast tomes of research on identity, and by necessity, as with everything in this book, we're going to have to simplify it a bit for accessibility. Theories of identity are hotly debated simply because identity is so hard to study, and so I'm going to say things that would get me tarred and feathered (or, more likely, passive-aggressively shunned) by some academics. But remember that our goal is behavior change;

the framework we use to think about identity needs to be only as accurate as required to help us change behavior. Otherwise we could write an entire book on the subject and still not have fully explored it. Book Two! (Just kidding, there will be no second book; please don't ever make me write another one of these.)

Because identity is the most powerful pressure, it is also the one with which we must be most cautious. I already spent an entire chapter on a soapbox about ethics and the process for addressing its challenges, so I won't belabor the point, but recognize that the moment you start involving yourself in how people see themselves and others, you take on an ethical responsibility that requires care. That isn't a warning not to use identity, as that's essentially impossible, because everything we do is tied into our identities at one level or another. Instead, try to think of it like driving—you're going to do it a lot and accidents happen when you go on autopilot. Buckle up and check your mirrors!

Typically, when we ask people about identity, they tend to focus on the roles they inhabit: I'm a dad. I'm a behavioral scientist. I'm a country boy. We have many roles and they aren't always in perfect alignment with one another, shifting constantly to accommodate our circumstances, both consciously and unconsciously. And that's actually the source of their power for behavior change: because our identities are flexible, they can create pressure where it is needed.

As behavioral scientists, we have to lean into that multiplicity. Engrave Whitman on your soul (and put it on your whiteboard):

Do I contradict myself?
Very well then I contradict myself,
(I am large, I contain multitudes.)

The goal here isn't putting individual people into buckets but rather to use the complexities of identity, as expressed through behavior, to reach the behavioral outcome we want.

So how do we do that? To start, let's get away from roles and their bastard cousins, personas. Nothing creates confirmation bias quite like a persona, because we are free to manipulate this rich imaginary figure to have whatever characteristics support the interventions we want to run. Personas are for modern Mad Men. And accurately mapping and validating pressures supplants the need for personas, as confirmed characteristics that actually determine behavior will always be better than imaginary figures.

Try to think of identity as hierarchy. At the top are the roles, which don't mean anything in and of themselves but are simply shorthand for a set of values that live underneath. These values are then associated with actual behaviors, because identity is really a sentence we tell ourselves and others:

"I'm the kind of person who [value/behavior]." When I say I'm a country boy, I am actually talking about a collection of behaviors and values with which I associate, commonly called my in-group. They can be affirmative (country boys listen to Johnny Cash, wear cowboy boots, like simplicity) or antagonistic (country boys don't listen to classical music, don't wear suits, don't like bullshit).

There are also, as you might expect, out-groups: the roles against which I specifically define myself. These aren't always simply the opposites of my in-group; I wouldn't call myself a member of the young girls' club, but I'm absolutely opposed to the old boys' club in ways that clearly modify my behavior. When I say I'm not a member of the old boys' club, I mean something affirmative (the old boys' club likes measuring net worth, so I don't) and antagonistic (the old boys' club doesn't like camping, so I do).

And there we have the beginnings of a two-by-two matrix (got to love a social psychologist): in-group affirmative, in-group antagonistic, out-group affirmative, out-group antagonistic. But you actually already know these groups: they are simply shorthand for the identity forms of promoting and inhibiting pressures.

An in-group affirmative is a promoting pressure (a reason to wear cowboy boots), and an in-group antagonistic is an inhibiting pressure (a reason not to like bullshit). Conversely, an out-group affirmative is an inhibiting pressure (a reason not to use net worth), and an out-group antagonistic is a promoting pressure (a reason to like camping).

This matrix makes is easier to fit identity into the IDP. During our gathering of potential insights, we can ask questions about the in-group and out-group roles for our population. We can then map the pressures associated with those roles using both links to values and the specific behaviors they create.

Values play an important role here, because they have a transformative effect on other pressures. This is actually the best way to explain why we end up with so many counter-rational pressures. For example, *cost* is always an inhibiting pressure, but when modified by a value to become *luxury*, it can also become a promoting pressure—or remain an inhibiting pressure, depending on the in-group and out-group roles of your population. Values are like colored glasses, acting on our perception to modify how we process cues.

It is tempting to look at roles and think of them just like personas—because a person identifies as X, they will always Y. That simply isn't true, because of our multiplicity and the flexibility of the roles themselves (plenty of country boys don't wear cowboy boots, and what is the difference between a country boy and a cowboy, anyway?).

That doesn't mean identity isn't useful. Remember, we are trying to change the behavior of populations, and we should never expect that everyone will react the exact same way to the exact same pressure all the time. Because identities have varying relevance in different contexts. Your religious identity is more relevant to how you organize your weekend; your gender identity is more relevant to what clothes you choose. And how personally relevant your religious and gender identities are in the context in which a behavior occurs (because relevance is fluid as well; religious identity might be more important in church, less important at work) is what determines the strength of the pressures.

Which actually leads to our first intervention technique. When a role and an outcome behavior are closely linked, using in-groups and out-groups is fairly easy. Because of the strong association, simply activating the identity will result in behavior change, with in-group/out-group and affirmative/ antagonistic determining the direction of the behavior and relevance determining the strength of the change.

The most common technique for activating an identity is priming: using the direct connection between an identity and behavior such that reminding us, either consciously or unconsciously, of the identity then affects the behavior. In a lab this is often accomplished by forcing people to think about their identity using simple interventions like asking questions ("With what gender do you associate and why?" or "What does being female mean to you?"), although there are also people who like to use incredibly subtle primes, like objects in the environment (a recruitment poster for a sorority; an invitation to a women-only event).

My favorite research example also happens to show why this type of intervention isn't as robust as it sounds. The study[15] itself is fairly simple: Asian women are brought into a lab and primed to reflect on either their Asian ethnicity or their female gender; then they take a math test. And sure enough, when you prime *Asian* they score higher, and when you prime *female* they score lower, just as their stereotyped roles would suggest.

The problem is that attempts to replicate the study, with the same design, have increasingly failed, because the association between the role and the behavior itself has become less prevalent. Priming really only works if your target behavior is directly and clearly connected with a well-defined identity that someone is willing to self-express, and in the intervening twenty years between the publication of this book and the original study, we've gone to war on the idea that women are bad at math and Asians are automatically good at it. We may not yet have completely won, but we've certainly reclaimed enough enemy territory that the prime often doesn't work because the association is weak.

It isn't that priming doesn't work generally; it does, if the association between role and behavior is strong. But what do you do when there isn't a strong, clear association between a role and the outcome behavior you're interested in? Simple:

you create one. Enter moderation and mediation, the two intervention tactics we can use to make up for the weaknesses of primes. Because if primes work best when there is a strong connection between identity and outcome behavior, then moderation modifies the strength of the connection and mediation creates one where it didn't previously exist.

For moderation, let's use the recent #LikeAGirl campaign by Always. The primary commercial starts with adult female models who are given prompts and asked to act them out. "Run like a girl!" says the director, and the models dutifully do an appropriately ridiculous, arms-akimbo run. "Fight like a girl!" "Throw like a girl!" The ad even mixes in an adult man and a younger boy, with the same result.

Then it shows how actual girls respond to the same prompts. They just run. Like a girl. Because they are girls and that just means running the way they normally do, like everyone else their age runs regardless of gender. The segment ends with an even younger girl, who squints and blinks into the camera, shifting nervously as the director asks, "What does it mean to you when I say, 'Run like a girl'?" The girl straightens up: "It means run, fast as you can."

I cry every single time.

Enter moderation. There is an existing connection between the identity of *girl* and behavior of *terrible running*. In order to change the behavior, we need to weaken that connection. It isn't a prime, which affects how salient an identity is, but rather a separate intervention that changes the strength of the association between identity and behavior. The brand does this nicely in the commercial through the director, who engages the adult women in a conversation about the association they just played out and its roots in puberty. The conversation is the moderating intervention and after it, when invited to take another shot at running like a girl, the women now run confidently because the connection between *girl* and *terrible running* has been dramatically weakened. That's moderation in a nutshell: run an intervention that either strengthens or weakens the association between a role and a behavior, so as to modify the behavior.

To show how mediation works, let me tell you a story about my mother. My mom is one of the kindest people I know and a tough country woman. She's got a big heart and strong convictions and isn't prone to hysterics. But when I was a kid, I could reliably make her burst into tears with a single intervention: trying to teach her how to use the computer. Every session ended in crying, no matter what the approach, until even a hint of a sit-down with a keyboard was enough to cause her to avoid me.

In addition to being a country woman, Mom is a career nurse, first as an RN in a hospital and then as a clinical nurse educator. She retired a few years back (and then immediately unretired and started teaching nursing), but the last job she held, for just under ten years, was in nursing informatics. Which is exactly what it sounds like: nurses and computers. What. The. Fuck.

How did my mother end up spending ten years of her life shackled to the electronic boogeyman of my youth, whose presence so reliably produced tears? It just doesn't make any sense . . . until you look at it through the lens of identity.

In the early nineties in rural Oregon, using a computer was flat-out incompatible with my mother's identity. She grew up in a generation where technical spaces were hostile to women, people without a college degree, and anyone who lived in the boondocks. All of those relevant in-groups were on the inhibiting side of the equation, and it was killing our behavioral outcome, because she defined herself as someone who didn't or couldn't understand computers. Part of the story she told herself about being Jo Wallaert was that computing was a no-go.

But it was more than that self-story, more than the inhibiting pressures. I was a young man in love with computing. My parents saved hard to get us our first machine and there was definitely no budget for the Geek Squad (which didn't even exist and wouldn't have driven out to the foothills if it did), so I must have reinstalled Windows 3.1 from floppy disks a hundred times. They bought that first computer, but I built every one after that. Customization, power, configurability, utility . . . I valued it all.

And therein was the problem. All of those powerful promoting pressures that were so tied to my sense of youth and masculinity just didn't exist for my mom. It wasn't just that she had identities on the inhibiting side but also that the identity characteristics I was highlighting as promoting pressures weren't relevant for her. I committed the cardinal sin of behavior change: letting my own identity lead instead of focusing on my population.

Her work changed what I couldn't. First there was moderation: inhibiting pressures were reduced, gradually, as computers became more prevalent in the hospital, not just for men with college degrees who lived in town but for everyone. There was a loosening of the association between the identity and the behavior that made it easier for my mom.

But there was also mediation, the creation of an entirely new motivational pathway by introducing a waypoint between a role and a behavior. In this case, the mediational waypoint was a simple value: care. In all of its computing-related initiatives, the hospital started incorporating patient-centric care, from pictures of actual patients to data about health outcome improvement to rich stories about how a computer was used to save someone. It was a brand-new association that was explicit: computing equals care.

This wasn't priming; the hospital didn't try to remind my mom that she was a nurse or a mother or a woman, because that was already highly relevant for her. Nor did it try to remind her that all of those roles feature caring as a value, because no moderation was needed. Instead, the mediation was in the linking of the computing (behavior) and the care (value), such that her preexisting roles now incorporated that behavior because they already had the value.

Mediation creates the opportunity for moderation, which creates the opportunity for priming. Once an association exists, you can strengthen it and then activate it. And when you do it right, you change behavior. By linking computers to care, someone changed my mother's behavior around computing such that she eventually transferred to informatics and changed the course of her life. That's work worth doing.

10.

OPTIMUM COGNITION

Time, money, and other limited resources are powerful pressures that shape our behavior, but none is quite so universal as cognitive attention. Think of your brain like a pie chart that shrinks and grows to express the total amount of brainpower you have. Now, I don't know about you, but my pie is definitely getting smaller: as a thirty-six-year-old, I get less sleep, am more stressed, don't exercise, and eat worse than ever before, all things that reduce my overall cognitive resources. And there are constantly new demands on that smaller pie: Bear is certainly one, but so is an advancing career, a decaying body, and a world that is oriented toward doing more every day.

START AT THE END

This is why your brain is a cognitive miser: it relies on biases and heuristics and cues from the environment simply because it is motivated to conserve your mental resources. And the greater the strain on those stockpiles, the more pronounced those tendencies become. The importance of reducing the world to a single resource is that it reveals a very basic truth: everything competes with everything else. Hence the $220 billion spent on advertising: if we focus exclusively on promoting pressures and use the bluntest tool we can find, behavior change becomes just a nuclear arms race to spend the most to yell the loudest and claim the largest piece of a dwindling pie.

For a product design example, let's pick on Facebook. For years the company oriented itself entirely around the desire to get ever-increasing amounts of attention (with accompanying terrible data metrics, like *time on site*). Even as it became clear that people were starting to use the site more than was good for them, Facebook repeatedly released feature after feature to try to claim more of their attention, contributing to that global arms race for cognitive resources against every other social network.

But what if it had pursued the opposite path? The motivation in Facebook's behavioral statement might have been something like "stay connected to others." Its strategy, if we accept attention as a measure of connectedness, was to constantly try to make us more and more connected by spending more and more attention. But Facebook equally could have made it less cognitively expensive to have the same level of connection as we used to have. Would that be a better product?

That depends on what you want out of Facebook, and that is really the crux of this deep dive. Despite my deep love for inhibiting pressures, the goal isn't simply to reduce our cognitive spend to zero for all behaviors. Instead, what we want is a world in which we spend the majority of our mental resources on the things that we care the most about and as few as possible on the things we don't. It is a sort of cognitive optimum for our Goldilocks brain: just enough cognition to keep us happy, not so much that we end our day exhausted for the wrong reasons.

Take the darling of inhibiting pressures, Uber. If getting from Point A to Point B isn't something you want to spend your limited cognitive resources on, it is a good product, because its focus on the removal of inhibiting pressures has made it incredibly cognitively light—not just to use but also in the removal of the burden of planning and worry that existed before it. It can be hard to remember these cognitive burdens once you've given them up, but if you end up in a city that doesn't have Uber, you'll have a sudden jolt of panic as you leave the airport: how the hell are you getting to your hotel? And where the hell is it, anyway?

And yet millions of cars are sold each year. Why? Because

some people actually like cars and are willing to pay the cognitive cost to drive them. And the very existence of my preference for an early 1960s matte black Lincoln Continental with suicide doors suggests that there is at least some context in which I might be one of those people. There are some things we want to spend our cognitive resources on, and it is the role of behavioral scientists to create a world of products and services that allow people to spend as many or few as they want on any particular behavior.

To do that, we need to be selective about how and where we direct a population's attention and that starts with good insights. Quantitatively, since we don't have access to their thoughts (yet; I'm sure any number of technocrats are working on it), we could look at where they actually allocate their time, money, and other limited resources and, when put under resource constraint, what behaviors drop off most quickly. Qualitatively, we can start to ask questions about their cognition, what trade-offs they make, and where they would like to be spending more time. But always take their answers with a grain of salt: as social psychologist Tim Wilson (borrowing from Nietzsche) put it, we are strangers to ourselves, since our nonconscious mind does immense amounts of the work and our conscious mind is filtering perception through myriad biases.

As we search for insights around cognitive spend, it is important to be specific. There is a difference between wanting to spend mental energy buying clothes and wanting to spend it picking out outfits or showing off wearing them. Think about Blue Apron's rise and stall-out: it sold investors on the idea that it would make cooking easy for people who didn't want to spend mental energy on cooking, but it actually makes cooking quite hard and mentally effortful. Reading a Blue Apron recipe is like watching *Chopped*: it uses techniques I've never even heard of. What Blue Apron made easy was ingredient and recipe selection, which is a noble pursuit but geared to a far smaller population of people who want to spend mental resources only on the actual act of cooking. Not exactly a billion-dollar business, or at least not the one it sold the world.

And worse, it isn't clear that ingredient and recipe selection aren't actually part of what makes cooking enjoyable— not because the activity itself is pleasurable (although it is for me: I like picking out the food more than I probably like cooking it and, judging by the number of fresh markets in the world, I'm not alone) but because the cognitive cost is part of the pleasure. In psychology we joke that the reason to run is so you can stop running; the removal of the effort is what makes it feel good. Our brain believes that the things we spend resources on must really matter, because we spent so much attention on them. So when you remove cognitive spend indiscriminately, you may actually lessen the subsequent behavior's enjoyment and thus how likely people are to do it.

Specificity around the exact things people do and don't want to spend cognitive resources on is part of avoiding the Blue Apron problem. We can also look at preferences for certain kinds of features (which also clue us in to potential interventions) that require more or less cognitive processing. For example, automaticity and curation. Because I don't particularly enjoy the actual process of buying clothes or picking out an outfit, my behavior is determined mostly by a desire to minimize inhibiting pressures, as long as the basic promoting pressure is high enough. Thus automation is an important feature for me; I actually wear the same thing every workday (40R John Varvatos blazer, Nordstrom Trim Fit shirt, John Varvatos jeans, brown or black Ariat cowboy boots) and built a script on eBay that automatically buys my wardrobe below a certain price, reducing my cognitive spend to near zero.

That way I can spend more mental resources on computers. I've built every desktop I've ever owned (except for the first one), and I like spending time thinking about each component, reading the reviews, and shopping for the very best price. I would never automate that part of my life and instead seek out curation: deep, thoughtful content and features that let me spend time thinking more about something I enjoy. Imagine a virtual configurator that lets you estimate the total computing power of a machine or interviews with noted system builders; those are both powerful curatorial experiences that appeal to someone like me.

Somewhere out there (beneath the pale moonlight) is my opposite. They want to minimize their mental spend on computing and would love a subscription service that just shipped them a new, unbranded computer every two years. But they care deeply about the buying, combining, and wearing of clothes, so they would never automate their wardrobe and relentlessly consume Instagram to see what's hot. What we spend resources on is a big part of our identity ("I'm the kind of person who takes time to find the best computer components") and we know how powerful identity is as a pressure.

Another difference in cognitive spend is where people put resources while making choices. Imagine that everything in the world has a secret, objective quality score. Book A is an eight, Book B is a seven, Book C is a five. Satisficing is looking for good enough. You have a minimum bar—let's call it a seven—and consider anything above that bar to be the same. If you look at Book C first, it doesn't meet the minimum bar, so you'll keep looking until you find Book A or Book B. If you find Book A or Book B first, you simply buy it and move on. This is highly cognitively efficient, but it means you don't get the absolute best.

Maximizing, by comparison, is about finding the best or

as close to it as you can get. If you get to Book B or Book C first, you'll just keep looking until you find Book A. And even once you find Book A, you have to go check out Books D through Z because there might be a nine or ten in there somewhere. Maximizing takes huge cognitive investment, but you'll be more likely to get the best.

In a perfect world, our brain would cause us to satisfice on the things we don't care as much about and maximize on the things we do. Unfortunately, it doesn't always work out that way, and it is relatively difficult for people to force themselves to adopt a strategy that doesn't come naturally for them. But as with automation and curation, we can build interventions that target these cognitive patterns. For example, if we're interested in a behavior like buying, limiting choice set sizes by offering only a few clearly differentiated products can be disproportionately impactful on the behavior of someone who is maximizing, as it means it is relatively easy to find the best.

Once you have insight into the cognitive preferences of your population, you may need to split the population into two or more as you drill down into the different places where people are willing to spend their energy. But this is where specificity and process help us. One of the values of the IDP is that it breaks down our products and services into smaller interventions that can be individually applied according to population. The difference between automation and curation is actually just one of interface: how many cognitive resources are people willing to spend on product choice? Everything else that makes a complete automatic or curatorial system is the same.

Imagine we take over Blue Apron tomorrow. We know that it is currently configured for people who want to spend their attention on the act of cooking, not on recipes or ingredients. We also know there is a larger population that wants to spend their resources on just the eating. Should we ditch our current population in order to pursue the larger new one?

Maybe, but that's a false dichotomy. We can simply spin up another brand, Green Spatula, with recipes that are easier to cook. Same ingredients, same outcome, just the slightly less tasty version that doesn't require you to have a vacuum sealer.

Ninety-nine percent of the hard part of operating Blue Apron is the interventions and systems that allow for a reduction in cognitive spend around ingredients and recipes: the acquisition in bulk, the reduction to smaller quantities and combination into kits, and the timely delivery of those kits before things spoil. Getting that right was hard, as anyone at the company will tell you, and spinning up a second kind of kit for people who want an easier option is a cakewalk by comparison. A shockingly large number of companies can expand their market dramatically with relatively small interventions built on the same infrastructure. But we can do so only when we are specific in finding insights around where our populations want to spend their resources and basing interventions on those insights.

Beyond the cognitive preferences and habits of your population, you should also consider the cognitive environment in which your desired behavior occurs, as it can change the pressures and thus the interventions. A choice made in a crowded bar is different from one made in a quiet office. Is your population likely to be tired or alert? Drunk or sober? Hungry or sated? All of these have implications for the amount of free cognitive resources they are likely to have and thus how they behave.

Harken back to the MacDonald paper[16] that I mentioned in the acknowledgments at the beginning of the book: alcohol impairs cognition, causing people to focus on salient (which really just means "obvious") cues in the environment. The general rule is that the fewer cognitive resources are available, the more your brain will rely on biases, heuristics, and salient cues in the environment. Which opens up new opportunities for behavior change.

Consider defaulting. Because your brain is busy, it will generally accept the default, even for decisions that we typically consider to be important. The canonical example is organ donation: in Germany, where the default is not to donate your organs at death, only 12 percent opt in, but next door in Austria, where the default is to donate, the rate is

99.98 percent.[17] But what if you ramp up the pressure? The more overloading the cognitive environment, the more likely people will take the default, so an intervention that either takes advantage of a naturally busy environment or creates one as part of the intervention and then follows up with a strong default is likely to create significant behavior change. Ditto for ramping up cognitive load and using strong, salient cues.

Lowering the cognitive burden of an environment can also change behavior by allowing time for a more reasoned approach. We know this so intuitively in the United States that we punish you less harshly for a murder committed in the heat of the moment (when your brain is overloaded) than for one that is premeditated (when you presumably had more cognitive resources to consider a different choice). Reducing cognitive burden can be a powerful addition to an existing intervention when a considered choice tends to result in the desired behavior.

Sometimes the interventions themselves are what trigger cognitive spend. For example, your brain is hardwired to attend to novel stimuli and ignore repetitive ones as a method of conserving resources. Manipulating the novelty of a behavioral cue can significantly change how we react to it and is yet another way to introduce additional strength to interventions.

We are dangerously into the territory where this chapter starts to become an encyclopedia of cognition, so I'm going to cut it off: get specific about where your population does and doesn't want to spend their resources, consider both their cognitive habits and the cognitive environments of your interventions, and spend that brainpower wisely. Done!

11.

UNIQUENESS
AND BELONGING

Humans are a pain in the ass. Cursed with complex brains, we are the Goldilocks of species, perpetually trying to balance a vast set of competing internal needs that go far beyond simple survival. And there is no set of competing needs more fundamentally paradoxical than the desire to both stand out and fit in.

If we don't feel special and unique, we get depressed. At the same time, if we don't feel like we belong and are part of a group, we get depressed. I call it the snowflake-in-a-blizzard problem, for reasons I hope are obvious, and attempting to

START AT THE END

solve for it eats up a shockingly large amount of our cognitive attention and determines an endless array of resultant behaviors. Because the world is full of threats to both our belonging and uniqueness, we constantly ping-pong back and forth between those two needs, trying to balance them out by investing resources in whichever is currently clamoring most loudly for attention. This constant attention makes these two needs fertile ground for interventions and learning to use uniqueness and belonging a key part of designing for behavior change. Take, for example, the modern log-in process.

When you log in to a webpage, what generally appears at the upper right? Your name. *Hi, Matt!* A nice trigger for feeling unique, as names are a big part of how we communicate our individuality in the world. Often you'll also have a profile picture, even on sites where a picture is completely irrelevant and used nowhere else other than to identify you to yourself. Of course, no one would ever say they log into a site simply to see their name and photo; that would sound crazy. And yet adding name and picture reliably increases log-ins, resulting in a behavioral outcome that is highly prized. Interventions don't have to be rational or things we'll admit to; they just have to work.

Lest we forget our need to belong, what do we see down at the lower left? Thanks to Facebook Connect, we can use a cookie to tell you that fifteen thousand people liked this book, including five hundred of your friends. Look how connected your tribe is! The homophily (*homo* = same, *phily* = like; the tendency of like things to group together) is strong with this one. And just as with the name and photo, nobody would ever say they log in to a site to see how many of their friends liked it, yet displaying how many people like something, both generally and within a network, is a standard feature of sites from Facebook to Pandora and beyond.

Making someone feel special can be as simple as customization, and increasing belonging can be as simple as sharing that customization (and ensuring it gets attention; nothing makes you feel like you don't belong quite like sharing something and getting no feedback). Interventions don't have to be deep to be effective; look at Coke and its cans with names on them, an easily scalable but uniqueness-honoring touch. For almost every intervention, there is an opportunity to add these two pressures and it is worth always asking yourself how you can integrate them.

Even as we strive for balance in individual situations, it is generally true that people are predictably more attentive to one side or the other at a global scale, and it is useful to ask yourself how someone with an imbalance in either need will react to a proposed intervention. One of my favorite lines of research is a series of studies done by Hazel Markus and her collaborators at Stanford on how uniqueness and belonging are viewed across cultures. Markus has shown that Western cultures, which generally emphasize uniqueness, tend to see themselves as making more decisions than their Eastern counterparts, who tend to concentrate on belonging. Because what could be more unique than individualized, agentic choice? For example, imagine that there is an array of identical surveys in front of you printed on different colors of paper. When you take one and start filling it out, are you making a choice? Westerners say yes, they chose a color; Easterners say no, the surveys are the same.[18]

The cultural differences don't have to be so stark as hemispheres. Even among Americans, people with higher socioeconomic status (SES) tend to be more oriented toward uniqueness than their low-SES counterparts. Why? Because when you're high-SES, you tend to be secure in your sense of belonging simply because you have what everyone else wants, so you spend your resources trying to differentiate yourself from other high-SES folks. Vice versa for low-SES: you already stand out, so you're looking for a tribe to fit with.

Markus has shown that this causes all sorts of interesting behaviors in a series of insanely awesome experiments.[19] But my favorite study by far is about car ownership. It might be because I come from a low-SES background (first-generation college-goer from the rural part of a state), but this is one of those examples that always sticks with me. So let's do it together, just for fun. Imagine the car you would buy if I gave you a million-dollar budget and you could get anything you wanted. What color is it? What make and model? For the book, let's use an early-1960s matte black Lincoln Continental with suicide doors. Chosen at random, nothing to do with my personal preference, of course.

Now you drive that car home and park it in your driveway—no garage, of course, because you want to show the world how special you are. And since you live next door to your best friend in the whole world, you sit and chat with them for a bit and just glory in that special feeling that is a new car. You go inside, feeling pretty damn good about yourself, and then sleep like a baby.

Ahhhh. You get up the next morning, stretch, put on your robe and go downstairs to get the paper, and maybe sneak a peek, just a peek, at the acres of chrome on that black Lincoln. And as you stretch contentedly, feeling like a badass, you happen to look over at your best friend's house, and what do you see but an early-1960s matte black Lincoln Continental with suicide doors.

How do you feel?

Well, it turns out it depends on your SES. High-SES folks spit nails, key that asshole's car, and start a range war worthy of the McCoys. Low-SES folks, on the other hand, start a car club. Because it is your best friend, and you want to belong, and maybe you could get your other friends on board and you all could get early-1960s matte black Lincoln Continentals with suicide doors and you'll all go cruising around town on a Friday night, the Early-1960s Matte Black Lincoln Continental with Suicide Doors Car Club.

It is important not to overgeneralize when it comes to demographics, and SES is no exception. Obviously not every single person is going to respond perfectly in alignment with their SES, and many people change SES over the course of their life. But if we're trying to change behavior at a population level, we don't need perfect interventions—if the outcome is the behavior we want, it is worth pursuing. So it is always worth spending some time thinking about whether the population you are targeting is more likely to be attending to their uniqueness or their belonging as your behavior plays out.

The effects can be powerful. Look at pictures of a Trump rally. Notice how everyone is wearing the same thing and saying the same thing? All you have to do to join is buy a MAGA hat and jeer and cheer and sneer at the right times. Trump's campaign identified a population with a need for belonging and then made it as easy as humanly possible to scratch that itch.

Then look at a Clinton rally. It is a celebration of uniqueness, deliberate and proud of the many different kinds of people it makes a place for. But did the campaign do a good job of making that uniqueness easy? Assuming it had the correct insight of the unmet identity need, and thus the strongest promoting pressure of its population, then the campaign needed to reduce the inhibiting pressures to honoring that need. Imagine infographics that celebrated the diversity of her supporters and a little tool that let you claim your little data point. Or even the simple sentence completion of "I support Hillary Clinton for president because . . . ," with handy tools for branding that uniqueness on your social media. If Trump was about an easy way to show off belonging, Clinton needed to be about easy ways to show off uniqueness.

Did a failure to translate pressures into interventions result in four years of the worst president our country has ever seen? Maybe. This book will be published as the next presidential race begins—now is the time to start drawing our arrows. What is certain is that just as a team of behavioral scientists helped get Obama elected, voting (and talking about voting) is a behavior that can be designed for.

Enough politics. We don't have to work just with existing populations, and uniqueness and belonging don't have to be just general pressures. We can actually refine our population, motivation, and accompanying outcome behaviors based not only on which need people are attending to but also on the valence of their reaction to a subject.

As a social psychologist, I make pretty much everything into a two-by-two matrix that yields four cells, and the uniqueness/belonging problem is no exception: let's call the aspects *stable* and *unstable*, *liker* and *disliker*. They exist along a spectrum, but for convenience I'm going to talk about them as if they were discrete categories. And because I haven't made fun of myself for a few chapters, let's use me as an example to explore. When my editor sent over the offer letter for this book, I sent her a turntable, speakers, and a collection of Johnny Cash on vinyl. It probably would have been easier to just say yes, but if we were agreeing to work together on something so incredibly important to me, I wanted to make sure she knew a part of what makes me who I am. Because "let the thunder roll and the lightnin' flash, I'm doin' alright for country trash."

My preference for Johnny Cash is part of my snowflake, the part of me that is unique and special. And as a consequence, I'm a *stable liker*—my feelings about Johnny Cash are relatively impervious to what others think about him or his visibility in common culture. I didn't like him more when *Walk the Line* racked up Oscar nominations or less when he made a commercial for Taco Bell. (If you're wondering why that might make me like him less, find it on YouTube. "Where else can you get so many choices for just a little Cash?" is just . . . oof.)

There are also *stable dislikers*. They're wrong, but they exist—they've engaged meaningfully with Cash's music and rejected it. Maybe they're purists and feel like he was derivative of Son House and Robert Johnson and others. Maybe they just don't like folk music. Whatever the reason, liking

Johnny Cash doesn't square with their identity and so they simply don't, in a permanent way. This is part of their snowflake, core to their identity and unmodified by popular opinion, just like my preference for Cash.

Then you have *unstable likers* of Johnny Cash. He wasn't a part of their identity at all until *Walk the Line* came out, and suddenly they buy the American recordings and declare themselves fans. Just as they did with Ray Charles before him and Edith Piaf after, as their big-budget biopics came and went. Unstable likers are honoring the blizzard, trying to be a part of something that other people are also paying attention to because that's the part of their identity that needs affirmation just then. It might be galling to some stable likers, who see themselves as the real fans, but it is just the other side of the coin and we all do it in different domains; seeking out a sense of belonging is important.

And of course there are *unstable dislikers* (otherwise known as hipsters). They don't care about Johnny Cash, they don't care about Johnny Cash, they don't care about Johnny Cash . . . and then boom! Walk. The. Line. *Heavily edited Hollywood bullshit! He's a sellout! Fuck Johnny Cash!* Too bad he was already dead and so by definition couldn't have sold out. But it doesn't matter, because just like unstable likers, they're in it for the belonging and the group and the shared hatred, until they find someone better to hate. And while they may feel easy to denigrate, unstable dislikers actually drive a lot of important creation: what is garage but a rejection of punk, punk but a rejection of rock, rock but a rejection of gospel? And that's identity in a nutshell; anything that can turn gospel into garage rock in only a few leaps is worth paying attention to.

It is important to understand that we are all a part of each group, depending on the subject. We invest in a variety of identity signals because it makes it easier to balance both needs; a diversity of stable and unstable likes and dislikes ensures that we have the flexibility to adapt to environments and our own changing identity but also benefit from the permanence of identity anchors in a changing world. For example, I'm a stable liker of Johnny Cash and can come back to his music through thick and thin, whenever I need to honor my uniqueness. But I'm an unstable fan of most authors I've enjoyed; I'm currently hooked on Richard Kadrey (who I hope appreciates all the cursing in this book). But to be honest, I probably won't remember his name in a year, given the rate at which I consume fiction and my tendency to ignore who actually wrote it.

So how do we find the stable and unstable likers and dislikers for our behavior of interest (or introspect about our own preferences; it's okay, you're not a narcissist, I promise)? After all, if we are going to start mapping the pressures associated with identities and creating interventions against them, we have to be able to target who is actually in that population. Fortunately, most of us can intuitively imagine ways to do this identification, simply because of the point I made earlier: we tend to spend an awful lot of our time, energy, and money on identity expression.

I'm going to ignore liking versus disliking, since it is generally fairly obvious and when it isn't, people will happily self-identify. The harder distinction is stable versus unstable, simply because of the stigmas associated with instability. The dominant message enforced about identity is that authenticity matters and permanence is the only acceptable authenticity. But that's horseshit. Think about your first bae: you authentically liked them but you knew it wasn't permanent. Yet the pressure was to say it was (I will love you forever!), and if you ask people about where they fall on the stable/unstable spectrum, they'll always crowd toward the stable end.

One easy trick is simply to ask about preferences that relate to the subject. You can tell I'm a stable liker of Johnny Cash because when asked what my favorite song is, I'll tell you it is a tough choice—obviously the American recordings remake of "Hurt," originally sung by Trent Reznor of Nine Inch Nails, is a powerful statement about addiction, and you can hear the raw pain of Cash's life even as he is singing someone else's words. Here is a man who has struggled with his demons and lost, repeatedly and for years at a time. If you watch the video, it has a brief flash of June looking down at him and it is such a sad image, because you know that she is conscious not only of Cash's frailty but of her own. If Johnny was fighting, it was June who was his sword and shield, and by the time of the video she knows she will die before him. Who will care for this man, she seems to say, when I am gone? She'll be dead in less than three months.

Or it could be "We'll Meet Again," the last song on the last record Cash made. He starts out by himself, but by the end his entire family has joined him and you can hear, between the words, them saying good-bye to their parents, both of whom are nearing the end of their lives. I can't think about the circumstances of the recording for more than a few seconds without tearing up, evocative as it is of my own singing cowboy grandparents, whom I heard sing that same duet in the quavering voices of the old and still strong, back before my granddad passed.

You feel the emotion there? See the length of those paragraphs? One of the signs of stability is a deep engagement, often with references to a personal connection to the behavior. It's equally true for stable dislikes. I'm a stable disliker of thin-crust pizza, and you better believe that I could explain why, chapter and verse (thick crust, BBQ chicken with lots of onions, just to be clear). Two quick tests I often use are the TED test (could this person give an unprompted TED talk about this topic?) and the beer test (would this person be willing to go out for a beer and talk about nothing but this topic?).

People talking about unstable preferences just sound different. They tend to trail off fairly quickly when it comes to discussion, because their favorite is the group favorite, their stories are meant for quick group affiliation (I swear I'm one of you!), and they are unlikely to relate the subject to anything deeply personal to them. I like the writer Richard Kadrey because he swears and reflects on the complexity and toxicity of modern masculinity while mixing in demons and jokes and trips to Hell. But that's about as far as it goes; I could probably fake a TED talk about Kadrey, but anyone from the stable camp would laugh at me.

Another easy trick is to look at self-signaling and social-signaling. If identity is the completion of the sentence "I'm the kind of person who . . . ," self- versus social- is all about who is supposed to be reading that sentence. Almost all behaviors are targeted at both but usually lean heavily in one direction. Someone listening to Johnny Cash through their headphones is likely more of a stable liker, while pumping it to the whole office is a social, and thus more unstable, action.

Another of the many biases we have as humans is that we tend to think identity is about the social, broadcasting to others your affiliation with a particular tribe. But if you think about our identity-relevant behaviors, the vast majority of them happen in spaces where no one else can observe. Whom, then, are we doing them for, if not ourselves? If you want to find the stable, special, snowflake parts of a person, consider what they do when they're alone. Yet another reason that triangulation between quantitative and qualitative validation is so important; qualitative researchers are good at differentiating between public and private behaviors, while quantitative researchers can use data from unfettered access to our unobserved moments.

You can see the differences in the public sphere as well. People with stable preferences talk to you; people with unstable preferences talk about you (taken personally, this tip could save you years of therapy). Remember what identity needs are being honored in each case: stable is more about yourself and unstable is about the group. So who are stable people talking to? Themselves (*ba-dum ching*!). Or, as is more likely, directly to the artist, brand, etc. that they are engaged with.

Unstable people, by contrast, are talking to one another. So while they may *@username*, it generally isn't in the first position precisely because they want everyone to see how much they like or dislike that subject. They need that message to show up in their followers' feeds, because how else can they get responses? They're actively recruiting for their interest, and for that they need a megaphone and some tribal signals of affiliation. I can't count all the people I've told about Richard Kadrey in the last month or so, but I've had precisely zero conversations about Johnny Cash (other than with my editor, who remains unconvinced, though I'm determined to wear her down).

There are plenty of other methods for identifying how stable someone's preference is and they're highly dependent on the behavioral sphere within which you're working. But even these few can actually point us to how to use the uniqueness/belonging dichotomy to change behavior.

Each of the four groups could be thought of as a different population that you build different behavioral statements around, with different outcome behaviors, pressures, and interventions. In general, we don't want the same behavior from each of the groups (and are unlikely to get it even if we do), so by starting to segment, we can flow with the tide of their behavior rather than against it. For each population, you can ask yourself, "What do I want from them?" and "What do they want from me?" and use those two questions to guide your process.

Let's take Microsoft and stable likers. What does Microsoft want from stable likers? To buy, and keep buying, its products. But that's true of everyone. What do stable likers have that others don't? A deep knowledge about the Microsoft experience and the opinions to match. If you're trying to create long-term behavior change, there is nobody quite like a stable liker to help you find novel insights, map pressures you didn't even consider, and pilot your interventions.

That's why Microsoft has the Insiders programs. Windows Insider, for example, allows stable likers of Windows to engage directly with Microsoft as a brand. They get prerelease versions of the operating system, report bugs, and communicate directly with the Windows engineering team. More than sixteen million people have participated, and they generate petabytes (aka lots) of data every day. Try to imagine the equivalent number of quality-assurance testers you would need to employ to get the same coverage and you can see how "use a beta version of Windows" might be a very valuable outcome behavior, given that they're working for free.

And the best part? This is what stable likers want! If you are a stable liker of Microsoft, talking directly to the engineers and being involved in the process of creating the thing you like is precisely the kind of access you want, because it operationalizes your knowledge and deep engagement with the product. Unstable likers would have wanted a picture with Johnny Cash, anything they can brag about on social media and show off to the world and recruit others around. I would have wanted to take a walk with the man and just talk.

Stable dislikers can also be used to discover insights and pressures, because they also have deep engagement with a subject, even if it is negative in conclusion. One of the off-shoots of confirmation bias and our tendency to focus on promoting pressures when increasing behavior is the tendency to talk to the people who are already positively engaged. But the people who aren't doing something (in a considered way) can be just as valuable for understanding behaviors. After all, who better than a stable disliker to identify the inhibiting pressures that tend to be our blind spot?

And odd as it may seem, stable dislikers also want direct engagement. It is easy to get blinded by their dislike, but remember: they have chosen to form a stable identity around this subject. I am a stable disliker of a whole cabal of smart conservatives, but I'd still expend resources for the chance to take a walk with one and have a thorough conversation about where and why we differ. It would affirm my dislike and what makes me *me* at some core level, and that's a perfectly fine motivation when what you want is perspective.

Unstable likers have a unique behavior that we also create interventions around: because they are trying to build their tribe, they are natural-born recruiters. Stable likers aren't as useful here, because they aren't as concerned with what others think. But unstable likers love referral programs, buttons for social sharing, factoid-style content, and anything that allows them to actively share their temporary love of whatever. It can't be deep; that's a turnoff, as it highlights their unstable nature, and remember, nobody wants to be confronted with the reality that their preferences are impermanent. But as long as it supports their sense of belonging, unstable likers are all in.

Be warned! You have to be cautious of people with unstable preferences (once again, taken personally, more therapy avoided). Because their primary drive is belonging, they're much more sensitive to the herd than their stable counterparts. Which means that if whatever group they want to be a part of happens to be made up of dislikers, they'll drop you like a hot potato. As pointed out previously, this instability is actually good for our society as a whole, but if you were heavily invested in punk when everyone transitioned to garage, you could find yourself holding a lot of studded collars that you just couldn't sell. Double down on continuous monitoring for any unstable intervention.

But what about unstable dislikers? After all, they are unlikely to buy in to your primary behavioral statement, and yet you can't ignore them, because they are out there vocally recruiting an army of haters to join them in disliking you. In reality, this is mostly about the other frame of reference that I mentioned early on in the book; sometimes we want to eliminate behaviors, which means strengthening inhibiting pressures and weakening promoting pressures.

If the dominant promoting pressure of unstable likers is finding a group that embraces them, then one of the most effective ways to silence them is to show them that their behavior is unacceptable to the vast majority of the population. Which is why I love the Target social media team. Not the real one, although I'm sure they're lovely as well, but "Ask ForHelp," a fake Facebook account created by Mike Melgaard in 2015. Target had just announced a new policy to no longer segregate the toy aisles by gender, a move broadly met with acclaim but that also brought out unstable dislikers who just had to let the world know how much they loved gender norms. Because who doesn't love a bunch of angry conservatives looking to find a sense of belonging and people who will agree with them? Good times.

After uploading the Target logo as his icon, Melgaard used the fake account to respond to the unstable dislikers on Target's Facebook page as if he were the brand's customer service team. Except instead of pandering to them, he mocked them, effectively shutting out any sense of community that might have grown around the pro-gender-norm commenters. His humorous responses got hundreds of likes before Target managed to have them taken down, while the rantings of the unstable likers typically received single digits.

A fairly representative exchange: Bronson Smith (and yes, sic for the whole thing): "so customers are supposed to waste time trying to find the right area to find the right clothes? Is this the same for the mens an women dept? Soon Target will have unisex restrooms. . . . . GLAD I DO NOT SHOP AT TARGET!!!"

To which Melgaard responded, "We're equally glad that you do not shop at Target, Bronson."

Should a real customer service department act this way? Probably not. But the result was undeniable: deprived of a community of other unstable likers, most commenters were promptly silenced and went back to quietly not shopping at Target, a perfectly acceptable behavioral outcome for an unstable disliker. Remember, interventions should be judged by their outcomes, and with unstable dislikers, silence is a decent outcome. And earning the respect of unstable likers who were in favor of the policy was a nice bonus. This is why being specific about population in your behavioral statement can be so powerful: not everyone needs to have the same behavioral outcome. And you never know; when public opinion gets strong enough, you might just flip a few unstable dislikers. If you chart public opinion around marriage equality, there was a pretty rapid swing as soon as it became clear that it was going to become a reality. Nobody wants to be on the losing side (unless they're specifically trying to belong to the losing side, which is a whole different hipstery problem).

Let me leave you with two additional tricks that can help make it easier to operationalize uniqueness and belonging on your team. First, you can focus your qualitative and quantitative researchers around these four identities to help make sure you're avoiding blind spots. Just as the competing pressures arrows help us to structure our work and find what we otherwise might have missed, you can literally draw out the four boxes of the matrix and make sure that each of them is getting filled in as your team goes through the potential insights phase of their work.

And then, as you're mapping your pressures and designing interventions, you can use each identity as a lens to keep the process moving. Being careful to avoid personas and stereotypes, encourage the team to each take on a role and actually try to discuss the behavioral outcome. How will each of them react? What can you learn from that reaction and how can you modify it?

12.

SPECIAL FACTORS OF INHIBITING PRESSURES

Before starting this chapter, I have to admit my bias: I love inhibiting pressures. I had to try really hard during Part 1 to stay neutral, to love all my children equally and do right by you by showing both arrows. But let's be clear: inhibiting > promoting.

Part of it is identity related. Mad Men fucking love promoting pressures and I don't love Mad Men (if you're reading these deep dives in order, Mad Men are my highly relevant out-group, making promoting pressures an out-group affirmative). I also like the ethical straightforwardness of inhibiting pressures: because people still have to originate the motivation, changing inhibiting pressures only changes the behavior of people who already want to do something. But I also fundamentally believe that inhibiting pressures in general have special properties that make them abnormally effective and that is the focus of this deep dive.

That "in general" clause is important. As with absolutely anything involving behavior change, it is not true that every inhibiting pressure is better than every promoting pressure or that all inhibiting pressures have the same special properties. If it were, we wouldn't need to generate insights and interventions that targeted both sets of pressures, and this book would be dramatically shorter. When you're reading through these special properties, try to think of them as additional ways to bring focus to an area that has lacked attention, not a reason to abandon the entire IDP.

First, a quick review of the one special property that did end up in Part 1. Because we typically are creating behavioral statements that are about getting people to do something more and not less, we have a natural tendency to gravitate toward promoting pressures. Which means that one of the reasons focusing on inhibiting pressures tends to be so powerful is that it is the set of pressures we have most likely ignored. This ignorance means it is fertile ground for new interventions.

I don't mean "new" as in simply novelty for the sake of

novelty; our lack of attention to inhibiting pressures means there is likely low-hanging fruit on that side of the equation. Because of all the interventions in the world that focus on promoting pressures, it ends up a crowded space, which means that effectiveness is reduced because you have to try harder for smaller behavior changes. Look at advertising. If yours were the only product in the world, advertising would be highly effective. But when you're trying to be more clever and interesting and unique than every other ad, you're paying more ($220 billion more) with less certainty.

With inhibiting pressures, it is easier to be distinctive and to stand out in ways that significantly change behavior. Take Uber. To be more beautiful than every other app out there, it would have needed hundreds of designers and a ton of luck to happen upon the right layout. But because nobody was paying attention to the inhibiting pressure of the payment experience, a small intervention had outsized returns. Electronic payment was actually fairly easy to do, but because taxi services weren't focused on it, Uber made a distinctive impression. And as we learned when we talked about cognitive attention, being memorable can be a very important advantage for an intervention.

Making payment easier has another advantage: it is homogeneous. One of the problems of promoting pressures is that they don't tend to apply equally across people: one person is eating M&M's because of low blood sugar, another is

START AT THE END

eating because they are upset, and another is just after something sweet and delicious. But they are all affected by cost. They are all affected by availability. They are all affected by convenience. Inhibiting pressures tend to apply universally, which makes addressing them disproportionately efficient.

This homogeneity also gives inhibiting pressures another special property: they tend to have longevity. Not only is the reception of M&M's fun-oriented brand context specific (good at ballparks but bad for a romantic dinner), but it changes over time. Brands are forced to continually spend resources on new content to make sure that the promoting pressures are relevant given changes in population and identity. Even flavor profiles have changed over the years, forcing new formulations of what should have been stable pressures.

Inhibiting pressures don't date themselves as quickly. Cost has been an inhibiting pressure for as long as there have been M&M's, and it is likely to continue to be for the foreseeable future. And while the bar for what we consider expensive certainly has changed over time, the rate of change is glacial compared with the relative turbulence of promoting pressures.

Yet another benefit of inhibiting pressures is predictability. Because promoting pressures have a greater tendency toward variability in different populations and contexts, it can be hard to forecast their long-term value as an intervention. How much more delicious is the forty-second flavor of M&M? What unit would you even measure that with, other than the behavior of eating, which is affected by temporary pressures like novelty?

Inhibiting pressures, by contrast, often come with units attached. We have to be careful of the trap of thinking of measurements like distances and dollars as linear (it isn't true that losing a penny hurts one one-hundredth as much as losing a dollar), but even directionally correct units do give us greater control and understanding that we can use to power interventions. A dollar may not feel exactly like 100 pennies, but at least we know it is probably somewhere between 90 and 110 and not 2 or 2,000,000. And while that may not matter as much for pilots, greater predictability at scale can make or break an intervention.

The final reason I love inhibiting pressures is Nobel Prize worthy. Daniel Kahneman (and his partner Amos Tversky, who could not receive the prize posthumously but was a true partner in all the work) discovered a psychological construct we call prospect theory: equivalent losses hurt worse than equivalent gains feel good. What that implies is that a reduction in inhibiting pressure will generally be more effective than the equivalent addition of a promoting pressure, particularly when it eliminates an inhibiting pressure entirely.

As an example, let's use the penny gap. In your closet is probably a T-shirt you got free from some event, which you happily took home but probably don't wear. If I had offered to sell you the shirt for a penny, you would never have bought it, but because of the complete absence of the inhibiting pressure of cost (also known as free shit), you changed your behavior. Clearly paying the one cent wouldn't have broken your budget, any more than you would have bought the shirt for ninety-nine cents instead of a dollar, but the elimination of the inhibiting pressure triggered a behavior. On a pure size basis, promoting pressures require you to go big, while inhibiting pressures let you focus on smaller interventions.

Taken together, all of the special properties of inhibiting pressures may not seem like much in the face of a world that is so heavily geared toward promoting pressures. But when longevity and homogeneity and the rest combine like Voltron, it is worth falling a little in love with the inhibiting side of things.

13.

COMPETING BEHAVIORS

This is a true Behavior Change 201 chapter; believe me when I say that you should not attempt using competing behaviors lightly. And yet there are times when you will encounter a behavior that is seemingly intractable, with a long history of surviving despite prior interventions, and you might just need to employ competing behaviors. Or you work in business development or a related role, so your entire job is thinking about the interrelation among behaviors. Either way, we need to talk. Let's. Get. Dangerous.

The IDP is formulated to look at a behavior in isolation. This is deliberate, because one of the quickest ways to end up launching no interventions at all is to try to take in the entire scope of interrelated behaviors that make up a population. Competing behaviors is a twist based on a simple truth from our understanding of cognitive attention: at some level, everything competes with everything else.

You can't smoke and chew gum or take an Uber and watch Netflix on your couch at the same time. If you lower the price of your bottled water, people are going to drink less soda (why else do you think the soda companies own the water companies and keep the prices artificially high?). Every time we change a pressure or behavior, it affects every other pressure and behavior in some small way. Now, we're not going to go full-on Butterfly Effect here—down that path lies madness—but it remains true that all behavior is interconnected, and it behooves us to step back and think of it that way at times.

The fundamental mental backflip you have to make is simply that competing behaviors now require at least two sets of arrows instead of one. Normally, in a competing-pressures model, we increase promoting pressures and reduce inhibiting pressures if we want more of a behavior. But there is a second path. If we acknowledge that other behaviors compete, to greater or lesser degrees, with our behavioral goal, then it is fundamentally true that reducing alternative behaviors is part of increasing our outcome behavior. And thus trying to eliminate the alternative behaviors is a viable strategy.

This can be dangerous, as you have to be careful about

inadvertently reducing an overall pattern of behaviors. In startups, we often say, "A rising tide floats all ships," meaning what is good for the industry is likely good for every startup in the industry, because even if your market share falls, the size of the overall market increases. Conversely, if you try to eliminate alternative behaviors that are too close to your behavior, you may capture more market share but shrink the overall market such that you find yourself with less than you had in the first place.

Fortunately, this is where the IDP can help. When we start looking at a competing pressure, we essentially run an entirely new IDP focused on eliminating that behavior. But when we measure the pilots, instead of measuring the alternative behavior, we measure our true behavior of interest. Because we don't actually care if water sales go up, so long as soda sales go down.

Theoretically, we could repeat this process infinitely: one IDP for our outcome behavior, then an infinite number of IDPs addressing the alternative behaviors. But there are obviously diminishing marginal returns as we move further and further from likely alternative behaviors. If I weren't writing this book, I'd be sleeping, so that's a reasonable behavior to address. But the chances that instead I'd be skydiving are low, so an IDP there would be a waste. Picking the right alternative behavior is a little bit of a Goldilocks move: close enough that it is a viable alternative, far enough away that reducing it doesn't inadvertently tank your outcome behavior.

To avoid that conundrum, we don't always have to try to extinguish the alternative behavior; instead, we can co-opt it. My favorite example is the former war between Uber and Netflix, and the reason I love it is that it was a war that nobody realized they were in. There was no *TechCrunch* article, no passive-aggressive digs at each other onstage, no drama of any kind. They may not even have realized they were fighting. And yet war it was.

What did Uber want you to do on a Friday night? Go out (and preferably get drunk, so you couldn't drive home). What did Netflix want you to do on a Friday night? Stay in. Those are mutually exclusive behaviors, and so a battle was required. This is one of the hidden beauties of the behavioral statement: it can help you find novel competitors and potential partners, simply by seeing whose limitations, motivations, and pressures align and collide with your own.

Uber and Netflix resolved this through product development. Uber began delivering food (so it was fine if you wanted to stay in) and Netflix started doing mobile streaming (so it was fine if you went out, because you would watch Netflix in the back of an Uber). If they had really wanted to resolve the conflict, they could have given you free Netflix streaming while you were in the back of an Uber, maybe with zero rating of data usage brought to you by T-Mobile. These

———

synergistic bundles are potential alternatives to running an IDP war against your competitors.

Either way, these are big company tactics; if you're small, stay focused on running the IDP for your own behavioral goals. Creating competition where it doesn't already naturally exist is a waste of resources, and the whole point of starting at the end is getting more for less by focusing on why we do what we do. This is a right time, right place strategy.

14.

ELIMINATING AND REPLACING BEHAVIOR

Finally! I've spent this whole damn book writing about interventions that make a behavior more likely, because it was linguistically convenient and there are dramatically more situations in life where we are trying to change behavior to make it more frequent, not less. But eliminating a behavior is a valid goal, not just for prosocial purposes like reducing spending or improving health outcomes but also for the pure capitalists. Getting people to start taking Uber is to get them to stop buying cars. The rise of the iPhone is the death of the Casio.

At the most basic level, eliminating behavior uses the same IDP, except you are increasing inhibiting pressures and reducing promoting pressures instead of the reverse. And as with efforts to create more of a behavior, our pressure mapping will have that same predictable flaw: because we tend to focus on inhibiting pressures when we think about eliminating a behavior (punishments!), there is untapped upside in removing the promoting pressures that cause the behavior in the first place.

There is one other important quirk to eliminating a behavior and it is a doozy. Because we mark them as specifically beyond the purview of our interventions, the motivation and limitations in our behavioral statement often get forgotten in the later stages of the IDP. When we're trying to make a behavior more likely, it is important that we loop back to limitations as we reach the saturation point, in order to grow the market (as Uber did when it started accepting cash). But when trying to make a behavior less likely, we need to loop back to motivation.

The basic problem is this: if we eliminate a behavior without replacing it with something else, the motivation goes unmet and people end up finding something else to fill in that behavioral gap. And often that replacement is quite a bit worse. Just ask Cady from *Mean Girls*; sure, she stopped Regina, but because she didn't initially provide a pathway to honoring the teenage need to express identity, even worse behaviors sprang up. Hence the whole "break a crown and call out how we are all special snowflakes in a blizzard" ending; she had to eliminate the motivation to be a "mean girl." Nature abhors a vacuum.

Let's take a non–Lindsay Lohan example: smoking. There is no public health victory quite so stirring as the reduction in smoking, from a peak in the midsixties, when about half of adult Americans smoked like chimneys, to its current rate of around one in ten and declining every year as older smokers die off. Cigarettes were ubiquitous, psychologically and biologically addictive, and one of the single most heavily marketed products of all time . . . and now they aren't, all in about fifty years. Why?

In accordance with our bias, we started with inhibiting pressures. Since death is pretty much the best inhibiting pressure you can get, we put giant fuck-off warnings on the packages. We started picking off the places you could smoke, one by one, turning smoking from a public behavior into a private one. We put in place massive taxes (more than half of the price of a modern pack of cigarettes is taxes) and aggressive laws about how cigarettes are sold, including strict prohibitions against any resale that would threaten those taxes. And this barrage of new inhibiting pressures worked, to an extent.

But the reason we are where we are today, with a steadily declining smoking rate, is because of the more recent attacks on the promoting pressures. The most potent, of course, was the perception of smoking as cool. Think James Dean and the Marlboro Man. That's why most smokers start in their teens, when the need for both uniqueness and belonging are at their peak.

So that is where the fight began. If smoking was supposed to make you sultry and gorgeous like Marilyn Monroe, we'll run ads of what smokers actually look like later in life. But because later is later and we want to target teens, we'll threaten it right here and now. One of my favorite antismoking ads has no words. We see an attractive woman from behind. An attractive man notices her and begins to move in her direction, as if to ask her out. She turns and in profile is revealed to be smoking, causing him to veer away. The implication is clear: if you smoke, you won't get laid. And for teens (and absolutely everyone else), getting laid is a powerful promoting pressure. Reduce it and presto, you get less smoking.

And the cigarette companies can't rebut the ad because we've banned their advertising. In movies, magazines, TV, billboards, radio, you name it—in America, you can advertise almost anything except cigarettes. Take away Big Tobacco's ability to use the Marlboro Man or glamorize Virginia Slims as the latest weight-loss technique, and you weaken the behavior those promoting pressures create.

Or, if you want to go even more ridiculous, think about cartoon characters. In the lawsuit that eventually ended Joe Camel, the plaintiff claimed that in the four years following his reintroduction, Camel cigarette sales to teens went from $6 million to $476 million. Around the same time, a *Journal of the American Medical Association* study found that six-year-olds were about as familiar with Joe Camel as with Mickey Mouse.[20] Killing Joe Camel saved lives.

Win one for a focus on behavior! Except now we have a problem: no more cigarettes, but the population (teens) still has the motivation (to look cool). They seek something that has ritual and routine, that honors their uniqueness and yet fosters belonging. Maybe something that you can have a favorite flavor of, that has endless accessories, that you can trade with your friends, that lets you ask that potential bae for a hit? We killed cigarettes but left a massive, gaping hole begging to be filled. Which might be why Juul (the largest e-cigarette company) just took a $13 billion investment from Altria (the largest cigarette company); everything about the behavioral statement, especially the motivation, stayed the same except that the behavior was e-cigarettes, so the synergy was natural.

Thus the need for a replacement when focusing on eliminating a behavior. In ending smoking, we focused entirely on "stop smoking" and forgot that intrinsic need to give a pathway honoring the motivation, a "start *something*," giving birth to the marginal improvement that is e-cigarettes. Because ultimately, as much as we focus on behaviors, motivations are what matter. If we wanted to truly end smoking, we had to replace that behavior with something that helped teens continue to look cool and have a conversation starter (half of smoking is the social ritual of bumming a cigarette or a light from a stranger; the other half is using "Want to go have a smoke with me?" as a way of getting someone alone) before something else did.

I'll end on a quick counterexample, just to show you what happens when you do it right. A few years ago, I was approached by a team of physicians working on the problem of heart disease in Africa. To combat a bland diet (motivation), many Africans had begun to add a large amount of sodium to their food (behavior). So we went to war on oversalting, with a variety of interventions. But we didn't simply say, "Go back to bland food"; instead we introduced an array of non-salt spices that could be used to liven things up. Because ultimately, what they cared about was having food they actually wanted to eat; honor the motivation and you can eliminate salt, replace it with spice, and not worry about oil and sugar slipping in to fill the gap.

15.

MINI CASE STUDIES

This is the end. My only friend, the end. (Only Jim Morrison could make so much drivel sound amazing.) All that remains is these mini case studies, which are like the lightning round of the book, except the prize is knowledge and the game show host curses a lot. Because if the difference between a junior and a senior behavioral scientist is simply experience, then this chapter is all about XP farming.

The Good Samaritan

A certain man was going down from Jerusalem to Jericho, and he fell among robbers, who both stripped

him and beat him, and departed, leaving him half dead.
By chance a certain priest was going down that way.
When he saw him, he passed by on the other side. In
the same way a Levite also, when he came to the place,
and saw him, passed by on the other side. But a certain
Samaritan, as he travelled, came where he was. When he
saw him, he was moved with compassion, came to him,
and bound up his wounds, pouring on oil and wine. He
set him on his own animal, and brought him to an inn,
and took care of him.

LUKE 10:30–34

One of the more famous parables from the Bible is that of
the Good Samaritan. A man is beaten and lies injured, and
two travelers see him and pass by without helping before a
third stops to help. The third, Jesus suggests, is the one who
will go to heaven, for it is he who loves his neighbor as much
as he loves himself.

But what if the first two were just busy?

Jesus seems to imply that stopping to help is all about
some internal, identity-related promoting pressure: what
makes the third man stop is mercy and love for a stranger,
core values that embody how Jesus wants his followers to
approach the world. But a 1973 study by John Darley and
C. Daniel Batson[21] nicely illustrates how inhibiting pressures,

not promoting pressures, are often the key determinant in whether we stop to help people who need it.

In the Darley study, a group of seminary students were recruited to participate in an experiment they were told was about measuring religious beliefs. After filling out questionnaires about their level of religiosity in Building A, they were told to go to Building B to do one of two tasks: give a talk about seminary jobs or give a sermon on the parable of the Good Samaritan. In addition, students were told they were either a little early, right on time, or running late.

Here's the twist: on the way from Building A to Building B, the researchers had planted an actor who appeared to be in respiratory distress, slumped on the ground while coughing and groaning. That was the true measure of the study: when confronted with an opportunity to help the sick, what determined whether students would stop to help or step over the person and keep going?

The first possible determinant of who stopped was how the seminary students viewed religion and themselves, an identity-related promoting pressure. Perhaps those who resonated with the social mission of Christ or believed deeply in service might be more likely to render aid. Alas, no. Despite people's mistaken belief that goodness is some sort of mostly internal attribute (remember our self-serving bias!), helping didn't seem to be based on anything the researchers measured about a person's beliefs or character. That's one potential promoting pressure gone.

The second potential promoting pressure was the nature of the speech they were going to give. Surely students who were going to give a talk about the parable of the Good Samaritan would be more likely to stop than those who were merely planning to talk about seminary jobs. After all, the parable itself is about stopping to help someone who is injured and exemplifies a belief that all of the seminary students had supposedly committed to as a lifetime vocation; what better prime could you possibly get? The speech topic was a powerful potential promoting pressure—it was identity relevant, core to the beliefs of the person, and top of mind as they were walking across campus.

There is also a bit of cognitive dissonance (the tendency of your mind to change your beliefs to fit your actions) lurking in the wings. After all, the students supposedly not only believed in the lessons of the parable but also were taking action on those lessons. The need for congruence between what we believe and what we do means that beliefs should be extra strong, primed, and readily accessible to change our behavior when we're about to take action on them.

But the topic of the talk they were assigned had no effect on whether a participant stopped: participants in both groups were equally likely (or unlikely) to render aid. Despite being a strong promoting pressure, the Good Samaritan prompt didn't seem to be enough.

Why? Because as is so often the case when well-reasoned interventions go awry, there was a powerful inhibiting pressure at play, one so devastating as to overcome all the many promoting pressures in its path: timeliness. The less time the students were told they had, the less likely they were to stop to help. In fact, of the forty participants, only sixteen of them stopped to offer any kind of help at all. And in the condition where they were led to believe they were late, only one of the ten students stopped.

Take a second to think about that. Imagine these future religious leaders hurrying down an alley and literally stepping over someone in distress as they rush off to deliver a speech about how the secret to entering heaven is showing mercy to strangers. Only one stops, passing Jesus's test.

I'll admit to always being a little amused by this image. As with the mayor in *Chocolat*, it is hard not to see the tragic comedy in such a juxtaposition between our stated intentions and our actions. And I'm not laughing at them as much as with them: I've been the modern equivalent of the hurried seminary student a hundred times over.

The temptation is to judge them harshly, but think back to your own behavior: have you ever felt in a hurry and snapped at a laggard child or gruffly pushed your way through a crowd, things you would never do in a more re-laxed moment? Perceptions of lateness don't create the promoting pressures, the anger that leads to lashing out or the altruism that leads to helping someone. But as an inhibiting pressure, how late we feel in the moment is one of the strongest factors in modifying behavior. Time isn't simply seconds, minutes, and hours—it is also how we feel about them.

The Waiting Subway Rider

People hate waiting. Even as cell phones have made it easy to do the same thing on a subway platform that we'd likely be doing on our couch at home, we're still a remarkably goal-directed species that mostly views travel time as a waste. And thus every public transit system in America is hated by its riders, even when the quality of the service is high. For example, New York City's Metropolitan Transportation Authority manages to successfully maintain an annual ridership of almost 1.8 billion people, and yet to hear New Yorkers tell it, they might as well be waiting on the slow boat from China. Imagine, moving 1.8 billion riders and still being referred to as "failing." Hell hath no fury like a New Yorker who has to wait.

One can imagine any number of interventions that would make people more likely to ride the subway, everything from making stations cleaner (reducing inhibiting pressure; the MTA is already increasing the frequency of heavy-duty station cleaning by 30 percent) to providing live music (increasing promoting pressure; the MTA's Music Under New York program has been around since 1985). But the wait-time problem seems intractable; you can only make the trains run so fast, and speeding them up tends to be incredibly expensive and time-consuming. Modernizing the train signal system, which is a significant contributor to delays, is projected to cost about $40 billion over ten years and will actually slow down the subways while the work is in progress. Not a very attractive intervention, even if it may be necessary.

This is where behavioral design gets fun. In most interventions where we are trying to change behavior, perception is reality, because it is our perception that changes the behavior. Often perception and reality are strongly linked, but not always. And remember, we're outcome-focused: an irrational intervention is perfectly fine if it results in behavior change. What if we could make people think the subway was going faster and that they were waiting less, without actually changing the waiting time at all?

One potential intervention could be simply keeping people busy during their wait times. Across a variety of studies,[22] people's prospective judgment of time (how they judge time in the moment, while they're on the platform having a nervous breakdown) is heavily affected by how busy their brain is. We all know this intuitively: imagine the way time seems to crawl during a lazy summer day and fly by when you're busy. Could we simply make people's brains busier by adding distractions like television screens, interactive games, and street performers? A Houston airport did this when people complained about standing around waiting for their bags; instead of making the bag carousel faster, they just made people walk farther to get to their carousel, which made people feel like the wait was shorter.

Physical load has a similar effect. What about a pull-up bar or giant checkers set? I could get rock-hard abs and the time would fly by. Of course, it also might make me sweaty as hell before work.

But the real inhibiting pressure here is ambiguity (which, as a general rule, our brains hate). There's nothing worse than standing on a train platform, leaning over the edge to see if a train is coming and watching the crowd grow as your watch ticks down to that 9:00 a.m. presentation you're supposed to be giving. *Should I stay or should I go?* That tiny, irrational tickle of regret knows that as soon as you leave, the train will come, and then how stupid will you feel? Nobody wants to make a wrong choice, but all the choices are wrong, so they just sit there, paralyzed and very, very grumpy.

Enter countdown clocks. When you show people which train is coming and how quickly, they can make all those decisions in an instant; what was ambiguous becomes instantly clear. Which is why, even without speeding up the trains, installing countdown clocks makes people feel like transit is running about 30 percent faster.[23] And it isn't just transit. Disney and others put up signs that tell you how long you'll be waiting in line, and they almost always overstate the wait time, so that you're pleasantly surprised when you get to the front sooner.[24] Who knew time travel was as simple as eliminating the inhibiting pressure of ambiguity and creating a little joyous promoting pressure?

The Frequent Traveler

I had the rare pleasure of meeting with a major airline twice, the meetings spaced about a year apart. The first year, I gave the standard promoting pressures talk, so when I got there the second time, they were all ready. "We've been doing it and we've seen success," they said, "but we hit a wall with this one."

The problem, it turned out, was getting a specific population to check their bags. The airline executives had already removed all the inhibiting pressures they reasonably could think of: they'd eliminated fees, made guarantees about how quickly the bags would show up on the bag carousel, and had

START AT THE END

industry-low rates of bag loss. And this had generally worked across the board, with one major exception: business travelers. No matter how hard they tried, they couldn't get these customers to check their bags, and there were enough of them that overhead space was still a headache that caused delays.

So how do you get business travelers to check their bags? You convince them it is identity-incongruent not to. For everyone else, delays aren't a huge issue; if you're on vacation and you land a little late, it doesn't matter too much, since you're still on vacation. But when you have to get to a certain meeting at a certain time and your reputation depends on it (because, given the lovely self-serving bias, being late is a reflection on your character rather than circumstance), then efficiency gets rather staunchly incorporated into your self-identity. "I'm the kind of person who is efficient" brings to mind George Clooney's character in *Up in the Air*, wearing just the right shoes to fly through security lines.

So by connecting "I check my bag" to "I am efficient," you get a lovely strong promoting pressure and subsequent behavior change. Think about that the next time you are watching airline ads or some of the subtle cues we now give you at the airport.

The Absent Flight Attendant

Another day, another airline. The problem they choose to workshop is simple: how do you reduce the number of flight attendants who call out sick? This, it turns out, is a major business problem because of FAA rules that prevent you from simply swapping in another crew. No one is allowed to work more than a set number of hours, so the entire industry performs a graceful ballet of shift scheduling that keeps the right people in the right places to staff the planes. Even one misstep causes ripples that cost real money.

We go through the standard exercises. Is the behavior really calling out sick? No, it is calling out last minute; with enough warning, the schedule can be adjusted. Okay, so we're looking at last-minute call-outs. What inhibiting pressures can be put in place? Force people who are calling out sick to do it publicly (social perception is a strong pressure). Make them check a box that forces acknowledgment that they are inconveniencing others, that starts with the word *I* to challenge self-identity.

A competing behavior is calling out early. How do you make that easy? Simpler form for early call-outs, harder form for last-minute ones. Early call-outs get a 20 percent rebate on the sick time. No public post for calling out early.

All valid, all worth piloting. But what was the intervention that did it? On-demand child care. After digging into the insights a bit, it turned out flight attendants had plenty of promoting pressure for calling out early and in fact wanted to do so; what resulted in the majority of the last-minute absences was sick kids and no child care. Subsidized on-demand child care was a benefit we had at Microsoft, so I was familiar enough with it. A short pilot later, we found out that the oh-so-predictable truth holds true: people want to do the right thing; you just have to make it easy.

The Yammering Product Manager

One of the useful forcing functions of behavioral statements is that they cause conflict early in the process to avoid misalignment later. Besides the fact that I love a good debate, this is a deliberate feature of the IDP: a good behavioral statement, especially with agreement on how the behavior will be measured, is what allows clear accountability for everyone involved and thus the ability to act independently and still be rowing in the same direction.

While at Microsoft, I got a chance to head down to San Francisco to talk through the IDP at the headquarters of Yammer. After I talked them through the pressures, we started working on a behavioral statement and ran straight into a quagmire. So I used one of the techniques that you'll find invaluable if you do this long enough: posit the extremes and see where people gravitate. The basic disagreement was over engagement (how often someone used Yammer) versus business value (how often they created something that helped the company). So I suggested the following thought experiment: *Imagine two people. One logs in to Yammer every day, chats it up with everyone, is highly engaged, but never creates any business value whatsoever. The other logs in only once, talks to only one person, but creates massive business value. Which one would you rather have?*

The room erupted in chaos as the two factions squared off and we were never able to resolve the disagreement (at least in that meeting). That's a bad sign for a company that had been acquired for over a billion dollars and was several years into scaling. And those are the kinds of fights you want to provoke early and that the IDP is designed for.

You may object to the phrasing: can't you have both engagement and business value? Of course you can. But you can build toward only one—the other is important only to the degree to which it drives the primary behavior. So for example, if all you cared about was engagement, you could reasonably say one of the ways to create engagement was perceived business value (a promoting pressure). If you cared more about business value, you could certainly say engagement was a component (again, a promoting pressure). But the fair that one is a promoting pressure to the other doesn't mean it is the only pressure.

And take this as fair warning if I'm ever judging a startup competition you're in. I will always ask what behavior you are trying for, and if you say more than one and I try to get you to narrow down, the answer "both" is an immediate down-vote. If you can't focus, you can't found.

The Underpaid Woman

Women are significantly underpaid and underpromoted in the United States. Ninety-nine percent of economists agree on this fact, but you're free to believe otherwise, just as you're free to not believe in climate change despite ninety-nine percent of climate scientists agreeing that global warming is the result of human behavior. You can believe whatever you want; you'll just be wrong.

I lead with this statement because if you are one of those people who thinks they know better than ninety-nine percent of economists, you probably won't like this section. If you want to be a better behavioral scientist, read it anyway.

We do feminism wrong (said every feminist ever). But it is actually true, and it goes back to that systemic bias toward promoting pressure. When women don't ask for raises as often as men, we just start layering on interventions that are meant to increase promoting pressure, like telling them to lean in or coaching them on self-confidence. And as usual, that means there is unrealized opportunity on the inhibiting side.

The backstory helps, so I'll tell it. When I was running product at Thrive (a personal finance website, Mint's biggest competitor, which we sold to LendingTree), I wanted to help people understand how well they were managing their money given what they had, not just create another credit rating where you get a high score just because you're rich. So in our Personal Finance Score, we had metrics like savings rate, which was based on what percentage of your income you put into an account and didn't touch for at least ninety days.

And when you look at it that way, women kick the shit out of men. Stereotypes about shopping are bullshit. The problem is that as soon as you take away "as a function of your income" and just look at raw dollars, women lose big time because they simply have fewer dollars coming in the door. And there is no budget on earth that can help you save enough to make up for the wage gap.

So in a subsequent project, we started to attack the problem of underpaying women. But we had one rule: no promoting pressures. The result was GetRaised.com, which has helped women earn raises simply by focusing on inhibiting pressures. Our outcome behavior was getting women to ask for and get raises. And instead of telling them to lean in, we started systematically removing barriers, mostly around effort and ambiguity.

GetRaised is, at its essence, just a giant Mad Lib. Answer a few questions and we'll tell you how much you're underpaid based on Bureau of Labor Statistics data. Then we recommend a raise percentage based on statistics about the optimum amount to ask for (the amount of the raise times the chance you will get it; at least in our user base, asking for an 8 percent raise is mathematically optimal). Answer a few more questions about what you've done and are going to do, and presto—we generate a letter that you can print out and hand in, scheduling a meeting and laying out the facts. Then there is a mild concession to promoting pressures: we start following up by email to track your progress and continually remind you to make sure the meeting happens. More than 80 percent of the women who hand in the letter get a raise and the average raise is over seven thousand dollars.

This inhibiting-reduction wizard format is actually a repeatable product template. For example, when presented with two job offers, women will generally take the one with a more certain payout. In certain industries, including tech, this means they tend to avoid equity in favor of salary, which is a problem because the only way to get fuck-you rich in tech is to take equity in a company that goes big. So again, we just built what is nothing more than a glorified calculator to reduce the perception of risk by calculating the expected value of equity. We don't track the results of SalaryOrEquity.com (because we run everything locally, rather than hitting the server), but at least in the low-tech interventions we piloted before building it, the results were positive.

You can also do the same thing to double the number of male feminists. I did some research with PayScale a few years ago that generated what I call the 3-1-1 rule: three in five men don't think sexism is real (assholes), one in five men see it both in the world and in their environment (woke), and one in five men see it as a problem in the world but one that doesn't occur within their sphere of influence (blind spot).

I don't know what to do about assholes, because they lack the basic motivation. In studies, the only thing that seems to work reliably is having a daughter. (Venture capitalists who have daughters are more likely to hire female partners and their funds have both better deal returns and better overall economic returns because of it.)[25] So if you've got an intervention for that one, feel free to let me know.

Woke men we can ignore, because they're already doing what we want. So then we have the blind-spot men: they acknowledge sexism is a problem but are less likely to do anything about it, because they don't see it near them. Is that a promoting pressure problem or an inhibiting pressure problem?

Both. IAskedHer.com focuses on promoting pressures by encouraging men to engage in conversation with the women

START AT THE END

they are emotionally- (and probably identity-) bonded to about their experiences of sexism. The goal isn't to put the burden of proving sexism on women but rather to ramp up promoting pressure by exposing men to proximal examples of sexism. Again, pilots were highly successful, because they challenge men's self-identity as someone who recognizes sexism is a problem to remain uninvolved in the struggles of close others.

WhyMenAttend.com is based on the results of a study about why men do and don't attend gender-focused events. In both cases, the behavior hinged on a promoting pressure: men who thought attending would make them better humans went; men who didn't . . . well, didn't. But right behind that, on both sides, was the simple act of invitation. Men who were invited went; men who weren't . . . didn't. Promoting pressure seems strong.

But then you dig deeper. Does an invitation increase promoting pressure? Yes, certainly. But it also reduces inhibiting pressure. Men who went cited the fact that there were male speakers and that the event description specifically called out that it was open to men. And invitations from women were more effective than invitations from other men, because only women are capable of establishing that the male presence is welcome and not an imposition. This is the power of small things. GetRaised, SalaryOrEquity, IAskedHer, and WhyMenAttend are all technically simple and use open data. Yet all have been effective at changing behavior. You don't have to be a giant multinational corporation with a billion-dollar war chest to do something meaningful; anyone can help us science our way to a better world. It just takes a focus on the pressures and a willingness to pilot.

The Snacking GI

Since we started with M&M's, it feels appropriate that we end here. But note that the historical accuracy of this story is disputed by Mars, so take it as potentially apocryphal.

It's 1941. The world is being crushed by the massive war effort. Food is being rationed and the American government is proactively encouraging people to plant "victory gardens" and save their scraps to preserve resources. Forrest Mars Sr. and Bruce Murrie are committed to the cause, but in a unique way: their mission is to develop a chocolate that won't melt when included in military rations. This is long before modern climate control, so MREs (meals ready to eat) need to be able to last months or years in warehouses, and the food has to be not only palatable but also restorative—huge inhibiting pressures for all the brands that have tried before and failed, like the chocolate deliberately made to taste bad so soldiers wouldn't eat it all at once.

Enter M&M's. Inspired by the British-made, nonmelting

Smarties that Mars had seen being eaten by soldiers during the Spanish Civil War, M&M's become the de facto dessert in MREs, and GIs are quickly hooked. Then the war ends. Suddenly chocolate is no longer rationed and candy consumption explodes. What will become of our heroes, M&M's, without their fat (pun entirely intended) government contracts and with a host of new entrants into the chocolate confection space? They'll sell more than $700 million a year in candy—or will grow to do so seventy-five years later—because Mars unwittingly reduced inhibiting pressures to candy consumption the general public never even knew they had.

During the war and just before, chocolate was so scarce and precious that eating it for fun wasn't broadly socially acceptable (hence Mars marketing his original Mars Bar as nutritious). But in the postwar boom, supply loosened and social pressure weakened as an inhibiting pressure. But chocolate still melts. People simply ate less of it during the warmer months, which meant sales slumped for at least a third of the year, which created another layer of cost pressure: people had more money, but chocolate was still expensive because in order to transport it before it melted, it had to be produced near the point of consumption. And those locations were even more limited, since only climate-controlled stores could sell it and that wasn't nearly so common in the 1940s. Candies that "melt in your mouth, not in your hand" erased all those inhibiting pressures overnight. Suddenly there was a chocolate you could eat at a ball game or a picnic. They melted eventually, but not nearly as quickly as their competitors, and good enough was good enough.

It took a world war to force the reduction of inhibiting pressures that changed the way we think about chocolate in the United States. But imagine if this book had existed then, and a chocolate company had written a behavioral statement and drawn the competing pressures arrows. Might it, instead of M&M's, now lead that industry, simply by focusing on the pressures that govern consumption? We don't have a flux capacitor to go back, but companies are still winning by being the first to recognize pressures that others don't. Payment never felt inconvenient until you took your first Uber ride. Renting a movie never felt burdensome until you first streamed Netflix. Swiping right never felt fun until you first used Tinder. Sucking aerosolized water laced with nicotine and blowing smoke like a dragon never felt fun until you first tried a vape pen (okay, maybe the dragon part you knew, because dragons are fucking awesome, but you get the idea). What new pressure will lead to the next leap forward? Will this book help you find it?

NOTES

1. T. K. MacDonald et al., "Alcohol Myopia and Condom Use: Can Alcohol Intoxication Be Associated with More Prudent Behavior?" *Journal of Personality and Social Psychology* 78, no. 4 (2000): 605–19.
2. Traci Mann and Andrew Ward, "Attention, Self-Control, and Health Behaviors," *Current Directions in Psychological Science* 16, no. 5 (2007): 280–83, https://doi.org/10.1111/j.1467-8721.2007.00520.x.
3. Matthew Wallaert, Andrew Ward, and Traci Mann, "Reducing Smoking Among Distracted Individuals: A Preliminary Investigation," *Nicotine & Tobacco Research* 16, no. 10 (2014): 1399–1403, https://doi.org/10.1093/ntr/ntu117.
4. FINRA Investor Education Foundation, "2009 National Survey: Respondent-Level Data, Comma Delimited Excel File," 2010, www.usfinancialcapability.org/downloads.php/.

5. Barbara E. Kahn and Brian Wansink, "The Influence of Assortment Structure on Perceived Variety and Consumption Quantities," *Journal of Consumer Research* 30, no. 4 (2004): 519–33, https://doi.org/10.1086/380286.

6. B. Wansink, J. E. Painter, and Y-K Lee, "The Office Candy Dish: Proximity's Influence on Estimated and Actual Consumption," *International Journal of Obesity* 30 (2006): 871–75, https://doi.org/10.1038/sj.ijo.0803217.

7. Laszlo Bock, *Work Rules!: Insights from Inside Google That Will Transform How You Live and Lead* (New York: Hachette, 2015).

8. Rona Abramovitch, Jonathan L. Freedman, and Patricia Pliner, "Children and Money: Getting an Allowance, Credit Versus Cash, and Knowledge of Pricing," *Journal of Economic Psychology* 12, no. 1 (1991): 27–45, https://doi.org/10.1016/0167-4870(91)90042-R.

9. Noam Scheiber, "How Uber Uses Psychological Tricks to Push Its Drivers' Buttons," *New York Times*, April 2, 2017, www.nytimes.com/interactive/2017/04/02/technology/uber-drivers-psychological-tricks.html.

10. Adam D. I. Kramer, Jamie E. Guillory, and Jeffrey T. Hancock, "Experimental Evidence of Massive-Scale Emotional Contagion Through Social Networks," *Proceedings of the National Academy of Sciences of the United States of America* 111, no. 24 (June 17, 2014): 8788–90, https://doi.org/10.1073/pnas.1320040111.

11. Inder M. Verma, "Editorial Expression of Concern: Experimental Evidence of Massive-scale Emotional Contagion Through Social Networks," *Proceedings of the National Academy of Sciences of the United States of America*, 111, no. 29 (July 22, 2014): 10779, https://doi.org/10.1073/pnas.1412469111.

12. Mike Schroepfer, "Research at Facebook," *Facebook Newsroom*, October 2, 2014, https://newsroom.fb.com/news/2014/10/research-at-facebook/.

13. Dan Ariely, Emir Kamenica, and Dražen Prelec, "Man's Search for Meaning: The Case of Legos," *Journal of Economic Behavior & Organization* 67, nos. 3–4 (September 2008): 671–77, https://doi.org /10.1016/j.jebo.2008.01.004.

14. Thanks to Tyler Burleigh, who works with me at Clover Health as a qualitative researcher, for the stub on which this is based.

15. Margaret Shih, Todd L. Pittinsky, and Nalini Ambady, "Stereotype Susceptibility: Identity Salience and Shifts in Quantitative Performance," *Psychological Science* 10, no. 1 (January 1999): 80–83, https://doi.org/10.1111/1467-9280.00111.

16. T. K. MacDonald et al., "Alcohol Myopia and Condom Use."

17. Eric J. Johnson and Daniel G. Goldstein, "Do Defaults Save Lives?" *Science* 302 (November 21, 2003): 1338–39, https://ssrn.com/ab stract=1324774.

18. Krishna Savani et al., "What Counts as a Choice? U.S. Americans Are More Likely Than Indians to Construe Actions as Choices," *Psychological Science* 21, no. 3 (March 2010): 391–98, https://doi.org /10.1177/0956797609359908.

19. Nicole M. Stephens, Hazel Rose Markus, and Sarah Townsend, "Choice as an Act of Meaning: The Case of Social Class," *Journal of Personality and Social Psychology* 93 (2007): 814–30, https://doi.org /10.1037/0022-3514.93.5.814.

20. J. R. DiFranza et al., "RJR Nabisco's Cartoon Camel Promotes Camel Cigarettes to Children," *Journal of the American Medical Association* 22 (Dec 1991): 3149–53.

21. John M. Darley and C. Daniel Batson, "From Jerusalem to Jericho: A Study of Situational and Dispositional Variables in Helping Behavior," *Journal of Personality and Social Psychology* 27, no. 1 (1973): 100–108, https://doi.org/10.1037/h0034449.

22. Richard A. Block, Peter A. Hancock, and Dan Zakay, "How Cognitive Load Affects Duration Judgments: A Meta-analytic Review,"

Acta Psychologica 134, no. 3 (July 2010): 330–43, https://doi.org /10.1016/j.actpsy.2010.03.006.

23. Kari Watkins et al., "Where Is My Bus? Impact of Mobile Real-Time Information on the Perceived and Actual Wait Time of Transit Riders," *Transportation Research Part A: Policy and Practice* 45, no. 8 (October 2011): 839–48, https://doi.org/10.1016/j.tra.2011.06.010.

24. Karen L. Katz, Blaire M. Larson, and Richard C. Larson, "Prescription for the Waiting-in-line Blues: Entertain, Enlighten, and Engage," *Operations Management* 2 (2003): 160–76.

25. Paul A. Gompers and Sophie Calder-Wang, "And the Children Shall Lead: Gender Diversity and Performance in Venture Capital," Harvard Business School Entrepreneurial Management Working Paper No. 17-103 (May 22, 2017), https://doi.org/10.2139/ssrn.2973340.

INDEX

absent flight attendant case study, 207–8
alternate behaviors, reducing, 186–88
Altria, 195
ambiguity, as inhibiting pressure, 204–5
apocryphal insights, 17
Apple, 41, 44
   iPhone, xvii–xviii
Ariely, Dan, xx–xxi, 64, 101
automaticity, and cognitive resources, 150,
   152–53
availability, 62–63

Ballmer, Steve, 24
Batson, C. Daniel, 198–99
behavioral statements, 27–50
   cascading behavioral statements, reason
     for having, 119
   defined, 28
   evolving, to meet internal or external
     shifts, 45–47
   first statement, clinging to, 45–47
   Microsoft Bing in the Classroom case
     study, 5
   mistakes in, 37–47
   no behavior, choosing, 41–42

novel competitors and potential partners,
   finding, 188–89
object and key result (OKR), similarity
   to, 50
   in planning, 47–50
   scaling of, 48–50
   timid statements, 42–44
   transparency and, 48
   of Uber, 31–37, 43, 44, 45–46, 47,
     48–49
   for uniqueness and belonging, 171–75
   variables of, 29–37
   vision statement, distinguished, 38
   wrong behavior, choosing, 38–41
   yammering product manager case study,
     208–10
behavior change, xv–xxviii
   behavioral science and, xix–xxii
   Intervention Design Process (IDP). See
     Intervention Design Process (IDP)
   stigma associated with, 83–84
behavior variable, of behavioral statements,
   30, 36–37
belonging. See uniqueness and belonging
between-subjects test, 106

INDEX

Blue Apron, 149, 150, 153
Bonobos (clothing company), 24, 25

Cash, Johnny, 164–65, 166, 167–68, 171
Chocolat (film), 201
Chopped (TV show), 149
Clinton campaign, 162–63
Clover Health
    ethical considerations in flu shots for
        black population goal, 87–89, 90–91
    ethics training at, 92
    intervention design and selection for flu
        shots for black population goal, 72–80
    practical insights and, 16–17
Coca Cola, 159
cognitive environment of targeted behavior,
    154–55
cognitive resources, 145–56
    automaticity and, 150, 152–53
    breaking down products and services into
        smaller interventions, 152–54
    cognitive environment of targeted
        behavior, 154–55
    continuous monitoring of interventions
        and, 119–20
    curation and, 150–51, 152–53
    defaulting and, 154–55
    Facebook and, 146–47
    insights regarding, searching for, 148–52
    maximizing and, 151–52
    novelty and, 155
    satisficing and, 151, 152
    specificity in determining where people
        want to spend, 150–51
    Uber and, 147–48
color, 57–58, 64
competing behaviors, 185–89
    alternate behaviors, reducing, 186–88
    interconnectedness of behavior, 185–86
    synergistic bundles as alternative to,
        188–89
    Uber/Netflix competition, 188–89
confidence, 116–17
confirmation bias, 19
continuous monitoring of scaled
        interventions, 118–21
    changing pressures and, 120
    cognitive resources, race for, 119–20
    interruptive alerts and, 120–21
    piranha effect and, 118–19

convergent validity, 5
    on ethics, 91
    for potential insights, 18–20
    pressure mapping and, 67
cost, 63–64
counterfactual world, xviii
counterrational pressures, 58–60, 63, 64
creativity, xv–xvi, 70–71
cultural differences, and value placed on
    uniqueness and belonging, 159–60
curation, and cognitive resources, 150–51,
    152–53
customization, and uniqueness, 159

Darley, John, 198–99
data variable, of behavioral statements, 30,
    36–37
deep engagement, and identifying stable
    likers and dislikers, 168–69
defaulting, and cognitive resources, 154–55
Disney, 205
Duckworth, Angela, xx–xxi

e-cigarettes, 195
effects size, 107
eliminating and replacing behavior, 191–96
    heart disease in Africa problem and, 196
    inhibiting pressures and, 192, 193
    motivation and, 192–93, 195–96
    promoting pressures and, 192,
        193–94
    smoking and, 193–96
employee abrasion, 100–101
ethical check, 83–97
    ethics rule, 87, 89–90, 92–93
    Facebook's intervention to knowingly
        show more positive or negative content
        on users' newsfeed, 94–97
    how ethical problem, 85, 87, 90
    identity-related products and, 133
    intention-action gap and, 86
    intention-goal gap and, 86–87
    Microsoft Bing in the Classroom case
        study, 8–9
    transparency and responsibility clause
        and, 91–92
    Uber's incentivizing drivers to drive
        longer than safe, 93–94
    what ethical problem, 85, 86, 87–90
external insights, 17–18

Facebook
    cognitive attention and, 146–47
    ethics of intervention to knowingly show
        more positive or negative content on
        users' newsfeed, 94–97
    likes, 158–59
Field of Dreams (film), 28
file drawer problem, 116–17
frequent traveler (checked bags) case study,
    205–6
Frito-Lay Flamin' Hot Cheetos case study
    behavioral statement of, 33, 36–37
    horizontal generation of insights, 22–23
    potential insight, 14–15, 22–23

GetRaised.com, 211–12
Glusman, Andres, 81–82
Good Samaritan (helping others) case study,
    197–202
Google, 6, 11–12
    Docs, 39
    psychological availability study and, 62–63
Grant, Adam, 21

Hall, Jonathan, 94
heart disease in Africa case study, 196
Heiferman, Scott, 81
helping others case study, 197–202
horizontal generation of potential insights,
    22–25
how ethical problem, 85, 87, 90
"Hurt" (song), 167–68

IAskedHer.com, 213–14
identity, 131–43
    advertising spend on, 132
    belonging. *See* uniqueness and belonging
    computer use example, 140–43
    ethical responsibilities and, 133
    as hierarchy, 134–35
    in-group and out-group roles of
        population, 134–36
    inhibiting pressures, 135–36
    #LikeAGirl campaign and, 139–40
    mediation and, 139, 140–43
    moderation and, 139–40
    pressure mapping, 136
    priming and, 137–39
    promoting pressures, 135–36
    theories of, 132–35

uniqueness. *See* uniqueness and belonging
    values, role of, 136
IDP. *See* Intervention Design Process (IDP)
inhibiting pressures, xviii, 54–56, 179–84
    absent flight attendant case study, 207
    in competing-pressures model, 186–88
    eliminating behavior and, 192, 193
    ethical straightforwardness of, 179–80
    generally more effective than promoting
        pressures, 180
    helping others and, 198–99, 201–2
    identity and, 135–36
    lack of attention paid to, 180–81
    longevity of, 182
    male attendance at gender-focused events
        and, 214
    Mars M&M's and, 61–64, 216–17
    Microsoft Bing in the Classroom case
        study, 5–7
    predictability of, 182–83
    prospect theory and, 183–84
    Uber and, 65–66, 181
    underpaid woman case study, 211–12
    universality of, 181–82
    waiting subway rider case study, 202–3,
        204–5
insight validation, 18–22
    assigning different validation types to
        different kinds of researchers, 19–20
    convergent validity, 18–20
    cross-validation, 19–20
    Microsoft Bing in the Classroom case
        study, 4–5
    purpose of, 21–22
    training researchers and, 20
    what you are validating, focus on, 21
intention-action gap, 86
intention-goal gap, 86–87
interruptive alerts, 120–21
Intervention Design Process (IDP), xviii,
    xxii–xxiii
    behavioral statements. *See* behavioral
        statements
    competing behaviors. *See* competing
        behaviors
    dualities in, xxvi–xxvii
    eliminating and replacing behaviors. *See*
        eliminating and replacing behaviors
    ethical check. *See* ethical check
    interventions. *See* interventions

INDEX

Intervention Design Process (*cont.*)
  Microsoft Bing in the Classroom case
    study, 4–12
  organizational behavior change,
    applicability to, 125–26
  overview of process, 3–4
  pilots. *See* pilots
  potential insights. *See* potential insights
  pressure mapping. *See* pressure mapping
    and validation
  scale design and. *See* scale decision
  tests. *See* tests
  validation. *See* validation
interventions, 69–82
  Clover Health flu shot for black
    population example, 72–80
  design of, 71–77
  for Meetup's spam problem, 81–82
  Microsoft Bing in the Classroom case
    study, 8, 14
  multiple interventions, selecting, 77–78
  optimum distinctiveness as goal in
    selecting, 78
  reducing number of interventions,
    78–79
  scaling down interventions, 79–80
  selection of, 77–82

Jackson, Michael, 127
Jesus, 198
Joe Camel advertising campaign, 194–95
*Journal of the American Medical
  Association,* 195
juice/squeeze statement, 114–15
Juul, 195

Kadrey, Richard, 166, 169, 171
Kahneman, Daniel, xx, 183
Kalanick, Travis, 31

#LikeAGirl campaign (Always), 139–40
likes, 158–59
limitations variable, of behavioral
  statements, 30, 34–36

Mad Men (TV show), xvi, xxvii
Markus, Hazel, 159–61
Mars, Forrest, Sr., 215, 216
Mars M&M's
  inhibiting pressures and, 61–64, 216–17

promoting pressures and, 56–60
snacking GI case study, 215–17
maximizing, and cognitive resources,
  151–52
Mean Girls (film), 192–93
mediation, 139, 140–43
Meetup, 81–82
Melgaard, Mike, 175, 176
Microsoft
  Insiders programs, 171–72
  netbook focus, effect of, 40–41
  Office products, 38–40
  stable likers and, 171–72
  vision statement of, 38–39, 40
  wrong behavior, focus on, 38–41
Microsoft Bing in the Classroom case study,
  4–12
  behavioral statement, 5
  ethical check, 8–9
  insight validation, 4–5
  intervention, 8, 14
  pilots, 9
  potential insight, 4, 14, 17
  pressure mapping and validation, 5–8
  tests, 9–11
minimum viable product (MVP) culture, 21
moderation, 139–40
monitoring scaled interventions. *See*
  continuous monitoring of scaled
  interventions
Montañez, Richard, 15, 22, 33
motivation
  in behavioral statements, 30, 33–34
  eliminating behaviors and, 192–93,
    195–96
multiverse, 13–14
Murrie, Bruce, 215

Nadella, Satya, 41
netbooks, 40–41
Netflix, 188–89, 217
novelty
  cognitive resources and, 155
  creativity and, 70–71

Obama, Barack, 24
objective and key result (OKR), 50
optimum distinctiveness, 78
organizational behavior change, 125–26
Originals (Grant), 21

Pandora, 159
PayScale, 213
Pearson, Charles, 16
personas, 134–43
physical availability, 62
pilots, 100–14
    defined, 100
    determining what to do if pilot doesn't
        create behavior change expected, 103–4
    employee abrasion, minimizing, 100–101
    Microsoft Bing in the Classroom case
        study, 9
    multiple pilots, running, 103–4
    objective of, 113
    "operationally dirty" manner, conducted
        in, 100–101
    primary advantage of, 111
    reasons for running, 111–14
    resource efficiency and, 101–2
    speed to market, emphasis on, 100, 101–2
    statistics used for, 104–10
    validation of, 9, 102–3
piranha effect, 118–19
population variable, of behavioral
    statements, 30, 32–33
potential insights
    apocryphal insights, 17
    behaviors, focusing insights on, 26
    defined, 14
    external insights, 17–18
    Frito-Lay Flamin' Hot Cheetos case
        study, 14–15, 22–23
    generation of, diversity in, 22–26
    large number of, importance of having,
        23–24
    Microsoft Bing in the Classroom case
        study, 4, 14, 17
    qualitative insights, 16–17
    quantitative insights, 15–16
    validation. See insight validation
pressure mapping and validation, 51–68
    both sides of pressure equation, focusing
        on, 64–67
    context of pressures, 63–64
    counterrational pressures, 58–60, 63, 64
    eliminating behavior and, 192
    identity-related products and, 136
    inhibiting pressures. See inhibiting
        pressures
    Mars M&M's example, 56–64

Microsoft Bing in the Classroom case
    study, 5–8
    problems to avoid, 64–68
    promoting pressures. See promoting
        pressures
    Uber and, 65–66
priming, 137–39
promoting pressures, xviii, 54–60
    absent flight attendant case study, 207–8
    in competing-pressures model, 186–88
    eliminating behavior and, 192, 193–94
    frequent traveler checked bags case study,
        206
    helping others and, 199–201
    identity and, 135–36
    inhibiting pressures compared, 179–80,
        181, 182–83, 184
    male attendance at gender-focused events
        and, 214
    Mars M&M's and, 56–60
    Microsoft Bing in the Classroom case
        study, 5
    sexism and, 213–14
    underpaid woman case study, 210–11, 212
    waiting subway rider case study, 203
prospect theory, 183–84
psychological availability, 62–63
p-value, 107–9

qualitative insights, 16–17
quantitative insights, 15–16

responsibility, and ethics checks, 91–92
Roosevelt, Teddy, 124

SalaryorEquity.com, 212–13
sample size, 105–6, 109–10
satisficing, and cognitive resources, 151, 152
scale decision, 114–18
    confidence and, 116–17
    file drawer problem and, 116–17
    juice/squeeze statement and, 114–15
Scheiber, Noam, 93
self- versus social-signaling, and identifying
    stable versus unstable likers/dislikers,
    169–71
sharing of customization, and increasing
    belonging, 159
Smarties, 64, 215–16
smoking, 193–96

snacking GI case study, 215–17
Snickers, 59–60
socioeconomic status, and value placed on
    uniqueness and belonging, 160–62
statistics used for validation, 104–10
    between-subjects test, 106
    effects size, 107
    p-value, 107–9
    sample size, 105–6, 109–10
    within-subjects test, 106
The Streets, xxvii, 21–22
synergistic bundles, 188–89

Target, 175
tests, 110–14
    Microsoft Bing in the Classroom case
        study, 9–11
    number of people exposed to intervention
        during, 113–14
    reasons for running, 110–11
    refining intervention for, 113
    validation of, 11, 113–14
Thrive, 211
timeliness, as inhibiting pressure,
    201–2
Tinder, 217
transparency, and ethics checks, 91–92
travel time case study, 202–5
Trump campaign, 162, 163
Tversky, Amos, 183

Uber, 31, 217
    behavioral statement of, 31–37, 43, 44,
        45–46, 47, 48–49
    cognitive attention and, 147–48
    incentivizing drivers to drive longer than
        safe, 93–94
    inhibiting pressures, reducing, 65–66, 181
    Netflix/Uber, and competing behaviors,
        188–89
underpaid woman case study, 210–15
uniqueness and belonging, 155–77
    behavioral statements for, 171–75
    cultural differences in value placed on,
        159–60

customization and sharing of
    customization and, 159
deep engagement, and identifying stable
    likers and dislikers, 168–69
likes, use of, 158–59
population of stable and unstable likers
    and dislikers, identifying, 166–70
reaction to subject, matrix for, 163–67
self- versus social-signaling, and
    identifying stable versus unstable
    likers/dislikers, 169–71
socioeconomic status and, 160–62
websites logged into, adding name and
    picture to, 158
Up in the Air (film), 206

validation
    continuous monitoring of scaled
        interventions. See continuous
        monitoring of scaled interventions
    of pilots, 9, 102–3
    of potential insights. See insight
        validation
    pressure validation. See pressure mapping
        and validation
    statistics used for. See statistics used for
        validation
    of tests, 11, 113–14
vision statements, xvi, 38–39, 40

waiting subway rider (travel time) case
    study, 202–5
Walk the Line (film), 164, 165
websites logged into, adding name and
    picture to, 158
"We'll Meet Again" (song), 168
what ethical problem, 85, 86, 87–90
Whitman, Walt, 134
WhyMenAttend.com, 214
Wilson, Tim, 148
within-subjects test, 106

Yammer, 208–9
yammering product manager case study,
    208–10